# THE
# KINDFULNESS
# SOLUTION

*Transforming your body
and life through greater
awareness and self-compassion*

Karen M. Azeez

ISBN 10: 0-692-093230

ISBN 13: 978-0-692-093238


Library of Congress Control Number: 2018903466

Printed in the United States of America

# CONTENTS

Preface                                                           7

Introduction                                                      9
   Why is Change So Hard?                          9
   Kindfulness Defined                             11
   Going Forward                                   12

Chapter 1 - Coming to Kindfulness                                15
   My Story                                        15
   Sharing What Worked                             19
   Kindfulness Part One: Awareness and Mindfulness 20
   Kindfulness Part Two: Self-Compassion           21

Chapter 2 - Becoming Mindful                                     23
   About Mindfulness                               24
   Mindfulness at Work: Margie's Story             26
   Cultivating Mindfulness                         27
   Mindfulness and Removing Obstacles              33

Chapter 3 - The Self-Compassion Quandary                         37
   Why Are We So Mean to Ourselves?                37
   Self-Compassion Confusion                       41
   The Importance of Self-Compassion               45

Chapter 4 - Cultivating Self-Compassion                          47
   Self-Soothing and Affirmations                  50
   Gratitude                                       53
   Forgiveness                                     56
   Lighten the Load                                61
   Get to Know Yourself                            66
   Spirituality                                    70
   Fun                                             72
   Spreading Compassion                            75

**Chapter 5 - Greet Your Obstacles!**     77

Boredom and Lack of Purpose     82

Prejudice/Arrogance/Judgment     87

Loneliness/Isolation     92

Perfectionism     97

Procrastination     102

Unrealistic Expectations     107

Fears     112

Final Words on Obstacles     119

**Chapter 6 - Reaching Your Goals Kindfully**     121

Stake Your Claim     122

Assemble Your Team     124

Carve Out Time     127

Clear the Decks     129

Set Smart Goals     131

Use Gadgets, Tricks, and Tools     134

**Chapter 7 - Keeping Kindfully Healthy**     143

Real Self-Care for Busy Bodies     143

The Five Pillars of Self-Care     144

Putting it All Together     160

**Acknowledgments**     163

**About the Author**     165

# PREFACE

Writing this book may be the most foolish thing I've ever done.

That's because I truly believe that everyone who reads this book, takes its message to heart, and makes an earnest attempt to practice its principles will have the tools they need to lose the weight they've struggled with for years, get stronger, drop unhealthy habits and destructive behaviors, sleep better, learn to manage stress, and truly transform their lives.

Which means I may never work as a health coach or publish another wellness book or article again.

Honestly, if that does happen, I will be a happy woman. You see, I didn't set out to be a health coach and a wellness writer for fame and fortune, I did so because when I found a way to turn my health and life around I felt compelled to share it with others like me.

It might not be easy. There will be times that the ideas I present and the suggestions that I offer may bring up uncomfortable feelings or seem especially challenging. But please do not let that deter you. Instead let patience, perseverance, and gentleness be your watchwords.

Rome wasn't built in a day. But even more appropriate, consider this: It has taken most of us decades to become the people we are, so we should give ourselves at least a few weeks to undo some of that, right?

So, if and when you start feeling frustration, sadness, impatience, and even anger, put down this book, take a few long breaths, and thank yourself for doing this work. Then take a break, have something nice and hydrating to drink, maybe walk around a bit. And before returning to these pages, give yourself some encouragement. Although it might feel weird at first, I suggest saying out loud in a kind and loving tone,

"This will help me, so I'd like to get back this."

Yup, you guessed it, that's your first dose of the potent concept I've developed called "Kindfulness."

I've included much of my story and the stories of my clients as illustrations that people just like you have been able to transform their lives using Kindfulness. To protect the privacy of my cherished clients, I have changed their names and altered some of the non-essential parts of their stories (their jobs, backgrounds, etc.) But rest assured they do exist and continue to stay in touch, read my newsletter, and benefit from power of Kindfulness in their lives.

Let's keep our fingers crossed that this will be the last self-help book you—and many others—will ever buy. I've done my part by writing it…. all you have to do is read, be open, willing, brave, and take a chance on yourself. You deserve it.

# INTRODUCTION
## THE KEY IS KINDFULNESS

*"People have a hard time letting go of their suffering.*
*Out of a fear of the unknown,*
*they prefer suffering that is familiar."*

—Thich Nhat Hanh

## Why is Change So Hard?

So many of us spend years, decades, or our entire lives trying to achieve a happier life, more satisfying relationships, a stronger leaner body—and don't ever reach our goals. Sometimes we even wind up in a more difficult place than when we began.

When you think about it, we all know how to do the things that would improve our lives. Let's take weight loss for example. Diet books, fitness plans, DVDs, shakes, and meal plans all profess to offer some kind of magic bullet, but weight loss comes down to one simple concept: Expend more calories than you take in.

While there are myriad ways to do this, and I admit it can be much more difficult for some, depending on age, abilities, resources, time constraints, cultural background, metabolism, etc., the formula doesn't change. It's science. It's simple, yet it's seemingly out of reach for millions of us.

In our country today, obesity is a crisis. How can this be happening if we all know the solutions and are aware that carrying extra weight is risky for our health? The same question applies to dropping any destructive habit or adopting any positive lifestyle modification. Why is it so hard? Is it a sheer lack of willpower or time or money?

I've come to see that those just aren't the answers. I watched friends, family, and neighbors—men and women with tons of courage, strength, and hope, and those with all the resources in the world—fail at their goals. I even failed for many years to drop bad habits, lose weight, and get fit…until I didn't. Until something finally changed. And this drove me to help others, even though I wasn't really sure how at first. All I knew was that I wanted everyone to feel as good as I did, to have a second chance at life.

As I worked with client after client, I finally identified the key to getting past the obstacles, fears, and lack of motivation that seem to stop people dead in the track of progress.

And that key is what I call "Kindfulness."

Kindfulness is the potent combination of mindfulness and kindness to oneself/self-compassion that was needed to allow me—and later my clients—to finally shift away from the constant distractions of an overly busy life and a misplaced focus on caring for others, to real self-care and a sane and balanced way of living. Kindfulness is the key to pushing past the obstacles that block us from transforming our bodies and our lives.

# Kindfulness Defined

Kindfulness is not in the dictionary (yet). As you may have guessed, I made it up.

Like smog (smoke and fog) it's a combination of two words—in this case, mindfulness and kindness—to create a new word. But why do we need a new word when we have two perfectly good words?

Well, I believe that—just like smog—when mindfulness and kindness combine they actually become something else. Their combination is much more potent. Separately, mindfulness and kindness are two attributes that can benefit us all, but together they create the catalyst needed for real, lasting change that you will read about in this book.

Together, utilizing the enormously important attributes of mindfulness and self-compassion, we can finally overcome the deeply rooted behaviors and insidious belief systems that drag us down and keep us in a state of un-wellness. And we will have enough love and kindness for ourselves to take the uncomfortable and awkward steps toward transformation.

Tragically, we do not give ourselves the compassion that we freely give to others in our lives. Instead, we often ignore our own needs and communicate to ourselves in harsh and unforgiving terms.

But when we are able to become aware of and accept our obstacles, and apply patience and gentleness to remove them, the world opens up and a new life—with new, healthy habits—becomes not only possible, but almost effortless.

And that is why Kindfulness is the key to unlocking a world of positive transformation.

In the following pages, I am going to help you understand more about the power of Kindfulness, learn to identify your obstacles, and cultivate compassion toward yourself so that you can do all the things that you've wanted to do—in fact, known how to do—but somehow have never been able to achieve.

The good news is you've already taken a big leap toward this goal by picking up this book. It shows that you have an awareness that something isn't right or could be better and that you care enough about yourself to do something about it. Congratulations!

# Going Forward

Now, to keep up the good work...

Before you continue to the next chapters, I invite you to make three vital promises yourself:

1.  I will remain open to the concepts and suggestions within.
2.  I will be brave and honest when considering whether the obstacles described are similar to my own thoughts and behaviors.
3.  I will offer myself the same patience and gentleness I would a child learning to walk as I try to apply these principles in my own life.

If you are willing to make these promises, you are well on your way to practicing Kindfulness.

# 1

## COMING TO KINDFULNESS

## My Story

I wrote this book to share something that worked for me. And not only did it work, it worked at the lowest point in my life, when everything else had failed.

Once upon a time, not so long ago, I led a very busy life. I held a demanding full-time job, I looked after my husband and our beloved Border collie, paid the bills, planned our vacations, cleaned our apartment, cooked now and then, served my community, and often came to the rescue for my friends and family in crisis—I mean often.

I can't tell you if I was happy or not, because honestly, I never gave myself much thought. I do know that I wrestled with nerves and poor sleep now and then. I had muscle aches, gas, and cramps often, I lacked the energy I had in my 30s, and was slowly gaining weight each year.

Of course, I wasn't helping the situation. I had given up going to the gym because there "just wasn't time," and, as a New Yorker and a dog owner, I thought I walked enough anyway. At the end of busy, busy days, I took my comfort in comfort food, ordering in pizza, fried chicken, Chinese noodles, and cheesy enchiladas. Home cooking seemed like just another chore. I didn't see anything wrong with the way I existed. The funny thing is, I thought I was healthy—even with all those maladies. I just couldn't see it. I believed that sluggish, nervous, and achy was how one was supposed to feel at mid-life.

But then my already busy life became overwhelming and frightening. My father was diagnosed with bladder cancer. Once I heard the news, I spent any time off—personal days, vacations, long weekends—flying back and forth across the country to see him and accompany him to doctors' appointments and chemo or just try to comfort him in his pain and fear. I couldn't neglect my job, so I did my work on 747s and took business calls in noisy airport terminals.

During that time, my 89-year-old mother-in-law took a bad fall and her health began to decline rapidly. She bounced from hospital to rehabs, back and forth for months. My husband and I were facing the gut-wrenching decision to move her out of her home of 60 years and place in her some sort of facility. We were wracked with worry and exhausted all the time.

But our decision was made for us. In fact, in the space of just three weeks both my father and mother-in-law died. I felt like the war was over and we had lost. But I didn't realize I was not only defeated, I was a casualty.

By that time, my occasional nerves and sleepless nights deteriorated into extended bouts of anxiety and insomnia. I was 40 pounds overweight and felt achy and tired all the time. I had severe foot pain and irritable bowel syndrome. Worse yet, my entire outlook on life became very dark. I began to think about my own demise, obsessing about wills and funeral arrangements. I was only 47.

Thankfully, my story doesn't end there. No, it got worse. And that was great. Because sometimes we have to hit bottom to know that something's really wrong.

I was at my mother-in-law's funeral when I got a call from work. I answered it because I figured it had to be an emergency for my boss to call during a funeral, right? It wasn't. She asked if I could come in the next day because we had to decide on a paper stock for the annual report. I robotically agreed. But when I hung up the phone something had shifted.

That moment was my first wake-up call *(pun intended)* that something was seriously wrong. How could my boss be so insensitive to my needs? But then I asked myself the more important question: How could I let her do that?

I slowly began to realize that I was living my life for nearly everyone but me. I was spending all my time and energy caring for my husband, dog, job, family, and friends and where had it landed me? I was sick, tired, and resentful.

I had forgotten—or perhaps never knew—how to take care of myself. I had bought into the popular concept that self-care meant rewarding myself with a new handbag when I "earned" it, taking bubble baths to relax, and getting facials.

But now I was at a breaking point. I realized that if I didn't do something, my life would never change. People would continue to pull me in a thousand different directions; I would get heavier and sicker, even more depressed and anxious. This wasn't how I envisioned my life: sad, dreary, burdensome. It certainly wasn't fair, especially after all I had gone through. I wanted more, I deserved more.

Finally, I began thinking about myself, and having compassion for my struggle and for where I was. Without knowing it, this was the first crucial step on my own journey to Kindfulness.

After compassion came action: I eventually quit my thankless, toxic job, not really knowing what would come next. I just knew it had to be done, and that it would be OK if I leaned on my husband for a bit. It felt strange at first. I admit I had guilt and second thoughts. In fact, I often overdid it with other responsibilities. I would spend dozens of long, dirty, sweaty days getting my mother-in-law's house ready for sale to justify my unemployment. But it was a start and I realize now that's all that matters.

But when the house sold, I knew it was time to figure out the next phase of my career and life. Following my love of food and a long-held interest in natural health, I enrolled in New York University's Wellness Program and began studying nutrition, fitness, sleep, behavior, and stress management.

It was there that I stumbled on the second step toward Kindfulness: greater awareness.

In our nutrition class, we were asked to keep a log of our food. After a week I was shocked at the amount of fried and fatty foods I was ingesting. It was a powerful revelation.

I hadn't gone in thinking about weight loss, but I figured if I could cut out foods like French fries and enchiladas, I could maybe lose five pounds...maybe. I did—and I lost 10 pounds. I was encouraged and excited and decided if I started exercising, I might lose more.

The problem was, I didn't want to spend money on a gym and I was a bit ashamed to have people see me in workout clothes. But something wonderful happened: My desire to start exercising was bigger than these emotional blocks and I found a way to get past them. I searched the web for cheap fitness DVDs and began doing Zumba, kettlebell, boot camp, and other workouts at home, where only my dog could judge my sweatiness and lack of stamina. I cleaned up my diet even more, kept exercising, and I lost 36 pounds.

Not only that, "suddenly" my aches and pains were gone, my digestion was hugely improved, I was sleeping normally, and my anxiety was slipping away.

I truly was amazed that this could happen to a woman in her 40s. I was a new person, full of energy and positivity. I literally got my life back and I finally learned what it meant to take care of myself. I felt like I had found some sort of miracle cure and I just couldn't keep this discovery to myself. I decided I wanted to help others. I studied at the Institute of Integrative Nutrition and became a Certified Holistic Health Coach. But I didn't really understand what had happened and why until I started to help others like me.

## Sharing What Worked

When you lose nearly 40 pounds at mid-life and are glowing and happy, people are curious—they want to know the "secret." Surely, I had taken some magic elixir sourced from the rainforest in Brazil or bought a piece of equipment that allows you to lose fat and gain muscle in 10 sweat-free minutes. When I told them that I ate less and exercised more, they were utterly crestfallen.

That just couldn't be the answer. Nearly everyone has tried to eat better and get on track with fitness and failed in some way. I must've done something different. And they wanted me to teach them. Without intentionally doing so, I became the best advertisement for my health coaching business. People signed up for coaching sessions because they figured if I could do it, they could do it.

So I began to help busy men and women lose weight, get fit, manage stress, improve their sleep, and generally lead healthier, happier lives. From the start it was hugely rewarding, but it's never easy or straightforward. The first thing I learned was the truth of the saying, "You can lead a horse to water but you can't make it drink."

Each client came to me guns a-blazing, eager to change. And I would encourage them to do the things that had worked so well for me, or help them invent their own version. But inevitably, somewhere along the line, their will would dissolve. They would be seemingly unable to carry out the small, attainable goals we set toward their main objective. For example, they would resist something as simple as reading before bed to fall asleep faster.

Thankfully, I used these "failures" as an opportunity to dig deeper—to see what was behind their resistance.

And folks, that's where the magic happened.

## Kindfulness Part One: Awareness and Mindfulness

Just as I had identified a financial fear (not wanting to spend the money to join a gym) and pride (not wanting people to see me heavy and sweating in shorts) as my blocks to working out—and then found ways to work around them—I would help clients identify their own obstacles and give them the patience and compassion that I gave myself to soldier on.

I realized that these bumps along the road of their progress weren't bad—they were, in fact, the key to lasting wellness. They provided a golden opportunity to explore the emotional obstacles that had always held them back. Instead of accepting their pat explanations or excuses, we talked about their fears, perfectionism, unreasonable expectations, and other feelings that, unbeknownst to them, were blocking their attempts to take the simple steps to get healthier.

And I realized that if there were any "secret" to my success, any "magic bullet," it was at those moments. Because that's when the real change begins—an internal shift that allows the external actions to take place. This work is the first part of Kindfulness: greater awareness and mindfulness.

## Kindfulness Part Two: Self-Compassion

Once a client has a greater awareness of what prevents them from taking even the smallest steps for their own benefit, it's harder for them to "unsee" it. For example, if perfectionism is their problem then they become acutely aware of this trait when it pops up and prevents them from attempting to cook a meal at home or try yoga. Then it becomes more painful to surrender to this character trait than to actually try cooking at home, even if the meal doesn't end up being four-star restaurant quality.

Working on these obstacles can be tough for clients. It often brings out anger, frustration, and disappointment toward themselves. Too many times, I've listened to clients describe themselves as stupid or lazy or berate themselves for perceived mistakes.

Once again, I see this as an opportunity to make progress by offering them more than just an ear or a shoulder to cry on (which I do, of course). I also present them with ways to be kinder and gentler with themselves.

And that is the second part of Kindfulness: self-compassion.

Without this, I have found, it is nearly impossible to summon the courage and energy, and have the patience needed, to take those excruciatingly difficult first steps toward lasting change.

A wise friend of mine often says, "Change feels wrong." But more than that, change can be truly painful. Quitting smoking, giving up chocolate, or getting up earlier to work out can seem unbearable at first. The key phrase in that sentence is "at first." If we can just move through that initial phase of nearly unbearable discomfort, we are often home free.

How did I get past that first Zumba lesson when I could barely breathe after eight minutes? How did I give up bagels and cream cheese, nachos, and doughnuts when everyone else was indulging around me?

The answer was love. I found that I had learned to love myself enough to care for myself properly—not with self-indulgence but with real self-care, as if I was my own parent.

Now let's look at these elements of Kindfulness in more depth.

# 2

# BECOMING MINDFUL

## What does hunger have to do with cake?

I remember one of the first moments I realized I was living in autopilot mode. I was at a party and the host unveiled a huge and delicious-looking cake. Here's something that may shock you—I love cake. It's probably my favorite food and the sole reason I attend weddings. So when this scrumptious confection was about to be served, my mouth started watering and I could barely contain myself from leaping up and grabbing the cake cutter. I asked a guest next to me if he was going to indulge and he said, "I'm not really hungry." I laughed and replied, "What does hunger have to do with cake!?" Then I realized that I was really full, but was still planning to eat at least one serving of dessert.

I was a newly minted health coach, so I was accustomed to helping my clients identify moments when they could've made better eating choices. This little exchange got me thinking about all the times that my desire for a reward or a brief exciting sensory experience shuts out what is really happening in my body and eclipses my long-term goals (to maintain a healthy weight and eat nutritious foods).

I realized that too often my eating habits and those of my clients have very little to do with our hunger. In this age of overabundance, we grab handful after handful of pretzels during long business meetings, gobble popcorn at the movies, sip frothy drinks while we stroll, or scarf down a power bar in the car or on the subway, never really noticing whether we are hungry, still hungry, or full. We barely taste our food and therefore our stomachs and heads have little clue of when it's time to stop.

Clearly this behavior leads to all kinds of issues: overeating, weight gain, indigestion, and even diabetes. But if we slow down, pause, and think about our actions, appreciate and enjoy our foods, we can stop this behavior—and way of life—in its tracks. This is mindful eating.

Going back to that party. When I stopped and thought for a moment, I realized I just wanted a taste. I didn't want the sick feeling of eating an entire piece (or more) on a full stomach. I had two wonderful bites (actually the first was wonderful and the second was just good) and was satisfied.

That was my first try at mindful eating and my first foray into mindfulness—the alternative to living on autopilot.

## About Mindfulness

But mindfulness goes way beyond eating.

Simply put, mindfulness is a sensory awareness of our surroundings, thoughts, feelings, and actions. It allows us to live in the moment fully. We'd all like to think we live mindfully, but the truth is most of the time we are distracted by a swirling array of thoughts, fears, and desires— many of them completely disconnected to the truth or the present moment.

For example, have you ever been driving and realized that you have gone a pretty good distance without knowing it? Perhaps you were replaying an awkward conversation you just had with your boss. Your mind was certainly not 100% present for whatever was on the road. And if your thoughts were troublesome, chances are your emotions shifted to fear, anger, sadness, or frustration, and your body may have reacted with a quickened heart rate, sweatiness, nausea, or cravings for food, alcohol, drugs, cigarettes, and so on.

Unless we are about to crash into a tree, usually there is nothing about the present moment that should cause us this kind of physical and emotional distress. The distress is fabricated and unnecessary.

That's why practicing mindfulness is a great way to manage stress. It allows us to focus on what is real and happening now instead of constantly mulling over the past or worrying about the future.

Mindfulness is also necessary to provide an honest starting point if we want to change what doesn't work in our lives. When we slow down enough to identify and understand our thoughts and feelings, to make an honest assessment of our lives, to give up living in denial, it's easier to see what needs to be changed. Think about how many times you've heard someone say (it could be yourself), "I've got to face the truth about my weight and just get on the scale," or "I'll come clean, I joined a gym but haven't been in months." We associate awareness and honesty with good health or the beginning of a healthy habit.

My story, described in the first chapter, is a great example of slowly becoming mindful. When I hit an emotional bottom at my mother-in-law's funeral, I became aware enough to know that something was wrong with my life. Although I didn't really know what it was at first, it was a beginning. As I tuned in more, I became aware of my great discontent in my job and career. Because of this awareness, I was no longer able to tolerate it. Not knowing what to do next, I tuned in again and remembered how much I loved cooking and nutrition and wanted to go back to school. Getting honest about my eating habits then allowed me to see there was room for change in my body and health.

Perhaps most important for the purpose of this book, mindfulness allows us to recognize the fears and other mental blocks that are the real reasons behind our so-called failures to reach our goals. We learn not to accept our pat excuses for not doing what we know will help us, but instead pause to unwrap the layers of denial and dismiss them so we can move on more serenely and healthfully.

As we move through our lives with mindfulness, we become more comfortable living in reality. And we are more of who we are—including our quirks, foibles, and behavior patterns. Our actions (or inaction) and motives are no longer a mystery. With greater mindfulness we can learn to be in the driver's seat of life.

It's so powerful that I've seen it save someone's life—literally.

## Mindfulness At Work: Margie's Story

Margie had been diagnosed with breast cancer and lost her job in the same week. She was living paycheck to paycheck and didn't have the means to pay for costly treatments, surgery, meds, or whatever would come next. She couldn't fathom how she would scrape together the money for rent. She kept envisioning a bleak future of disease, homelessness, and death. She was about to give up and just let herself die. But a loving and spiritual friend sat her down and said, "Look around. You have a comfortable place to live today. You feel well and have strength today. Your rent and bills are paid today. And all we have is today. Worry about tomorrow tomorrow."

Repeating those wise words to herself got her through the day, and the next, and the next. Being calm and focused, Margie was able to apply for assistance, complete her treatment, and even find freelance work that was more fulfilling and lucrative than her previous job.

Whenever I get caught up in a whirl of future fears, I recall Margie's story, which she had shared with me to help calm me down. I look around and assess what I have, what is really happening, and what I need in that moment—instead of trying to do the impossible work of fixing what I can't fix in the future.

# Cultivating Mindfulness

Now that you know that mindfulness can stem bad habits, quell fears, and provide comfort and gratitude, I'm sure you're ready try it. But where to start?

Well, there are about as many ways to practice mindfulness as there are to cook an egg. And, as with eggs, it all comes down to taste and preference. Whatever feels right, quiets the chatter in your brain, and allows you to focus and appreciate the present moment, works. And whatever works for you consistently is the best choice for you. But first you will need to experiment with some different methods—maybe even using a combination of techniques.

To help you get started, here are a few popular ways to practice mindfulness:

## #1 - Breathwork

The simplest way to stop your head from spinning and get back to reality is by breathing. Breathing calms the entire body, quiets the mind, and can halt the "fight or flight" reaction. Everyone knows how to breathe, but for mindfulness purposes, the "4-7-8" breathing technique is a method that helps slow everything down and bring you back to now. "4-7-8" refers to the counts when breathing in, holding your breath, and exhaling. Here's how you do it: Start by sitting up straight in a comfortable position. Next, place the tip of your tongue on the ridge of your gums, just behind your upper front teeth. Expand your diaphragm and slowly inhale through your nose for a count of 4. Hold your breath for another count of 7. Open your mouth slightly, keeping your tongue in place, and exhale for 8 counts. Count each cycle and repeat as necessary.

## #2 - Body Scan

The body scan is another great way to increase your awareness of your body and promote physical relaxation. During the scan, you bring attention, in a very systematic way, to the sensations that appear in each part of your body. This practice can be done lying down or sitting, whatever you prefer. I wouldn't recommend doing this in bed because you might fall asleep. Unless you want to use this purely as a tool to promote sleep, then go for it! Try to find a quiet place with few distractions. Make sure you're comfortable. You can start from the top or bottom, left or right—it doesn't matter—just do one toe, finger, ear at a time (not in pairs). As you scan, begin to focus on the physical sensations that you're feeling in each body part before moving on to the next. Be curious. What does each sensation actually feel like? Try not to get hung up on why your arm aches or your stomach is growling. Just observe and breathe.

The breath is a key component of this practice. As you discovered in the previous section, conscious breathing has a tremendous ability to promote mental and physical relaxation. By bringing the breath to any place where you're feeling physical tension, you'll gradually release this tension. The physical release of tension then promotes a state of mental peace. Stay at each body site for two complete breaths. Breathe in a controlled, even, smooth, deep, and quiet manner. Breathe in and out as if the breath is coming from that designated site. A complete cycle of inhalation and exhalation counts as one breath. There are many guided body scans available on meditation apps if you feel like you need help at first. You can also do mini versions of this if you ever become acutely aware of pain and discomfort and you need relief.

## #3 - Reality Check

As described in Margie's story above, you can check off that all your basic needs are taken care of in the moment as a way to not only soften worries and fear, but to build a greater sense of gratitude and what is often referred to as becoming "right-sized." In times of crisis, we often focus solely on what is wrong. This hyper focus tends to magnify the problem and eclipse everything else in our life. Everything becomes distorted and unreal. But when we take an honest inventory of what we have today, in the moment, for real, our problems, our ego, our fears, and our disappointments usually shrink down to their appropriate size. For example: I am safe, I am employed today, I have friends, I am not dying, I have a place to live, I have food in my kitchen, etc. You can make these specific for work, relationships, or any situation that is causing distress.

## #4 - Grounding

Here you take note of what your five senses are experiencing in this specific moment in time: What do you see, hear, smell, taste, and feel? As you focus on what you are sensing, it brings you smack-dab into the present and out of the past or future. It's almost as if someone is waking you from a dream (or nightmare). Grounding is particularly helpful for anyone who suffers from post-traumatic stress disorder, because it takes you out of the intangible troublesome memories or unexpected feelings of fear and puts you squarely in the tangible present. Grounding can be done by anyone at any time. You can be on a crowded subway, in the middle of a work conference, or walking in nature, and notice the sounds, smells, sights, and other sensations around you. Be sure to engage all five senses, but perhaps most important, touch. Feeling your weight and feet can help alleviate the dizziness or flightiness that can come from anxiety. Besides inventorying the five senses, these are other quick ways to ground:

- Splash some water on your face. Notice how it feels.
- Sip a cool drink of water and feel it from tongue to mouth to throat.
- Yell, grunt, or growl.
- Stretch different parts of your body as if you were warming up to run or exercise.
- Rub your arms or legs.
- Get up and walk around; count your paces.
- Stamp your feet, and notice the sensation and sound as you connect with the ground. Moving the body to feel the ground (such as jumping or stomping) is often helpful to stop an unhinged feeling and calm the mind.
- Clap and rub your hands together. Hear the noise and feel the sensation in your hands and arms.

When you have finished a few rounds of this and no longer feel out of control, try to take note of your emotions and thoughts and speak them out loud. Again, this will allow you to stay real.

## #5 - Meditation

This is, in fact, one of the easiest, simplest, cheapest, and most flexible ways to treat and ameliorate a multitude of physical and emotional (and spiritual) conditions including anxiety, depression, hypertension, pain management, asthma, and irritable bowel syndrome, among others. A study for the National Institutes of Health showed that the slowed breathing and deep rest achieved through meditation sparks biochemical changes that help the body and mind reach a more balanced state, in turn triggering the body's own self-repair mechanism. There are more ways to meditate than you can imagine. You can sit with your eyes opened, closed, or somewhere in between, count your breaths, listen to someone guiding you, or even sing or chant a mantra—as long as you can sit and breathe you can meditate. It is a great way to give your brain a break and listen to your intuition. Many people incorporate counting and breathwork to get started. But there are a thousand ways to meditate including: guided meditations galore that can lead you through peaceful meadows and other relaxing environments; chanting meditations or ones using a mantra (repeated phrase or word); and religious, prayer-like meditations as well.

As with the other exercises described above, I recommended that you find a relatively peaceful place and a comfortable position that you can hold without moving for the duration (try five minutes at first). Hands on lap, feet on the ground or crossed, eyes closed or open—that's up to you, as long as it allows you to be distraction-free.

Practicing Yoga Nidra, a form of meditation, I learned to conjure up different items in a category or an item for each basic color—this usually gives me a clue into what's going on in my psyche. For example, one day I was doing the color exercise and my mind offered these examples: black cat, green monster, purple people-eater, brown bear... It doesn't take a PhD in psychology to see that I was afraid of something.

For those just beginning, try five minutes of daily meditation at first, then add a few minutes each week. Don't be discouraged by racing thoughts, scattered images, or losing count. This is all part of the process. No one—I mean no one—is able to achieve a purely blank mind. The idea is to slow down your thinking and try to dismiss thoughts, fears, plans, or worries as they come. You will see that even if you can't still your mind for more than one second, the time you spend in trying to meditate will be well worth it.

In Chapter 6, I mention some wonderful apps that can help you with meditation reminders and offer guided meditations. There are also great books, classes, and recordings available.

## #6 - Journaling

Writing your thoughts at the end or very beginning of the day without censorship or judgment helps clear the mind, allay nervousness, and may allow you to see patterns of behavior or thought. Many people like to do a stream of consciousness kind of writing exercise like the one described in the popular book "The Artist's Way," by Julia Cameron. Others keep more of a memoir or an accounting of their day and the feelings that arise. Whatever you choose, consistency is key. Therefore, try to carve out a specific time to do this each day. Make it a sacred commitment by buying a fancy new notebook, lighting candles or incense, or playing soft music. This makes it less of a chore and more about self-care and self-love (which we'll get to later).

## #7 - Gratitude Lists

Like the reality check described above, writing a daily list of what you are grateful for, from the mundane (think pumpkin spice latte) to the profound (a loved one), is a useful tool in helping us see our world as it is and defending against negativism. Many people I know create a gratitude circle and share their daily lists via text or email as a way to stay accountable. This also works to jog your memory for items you may have missed. You see, after about a week, it's easy to get in a rut, unable to find original things for your list. But if your friend adds her favorite sports team, a new pair of boots, the fact that her parents sent her to college, or that she didn't catch the flu, you might find you are grateful for these things as well.

## #8 - Hyperfocus

My favorite author on this subject is Thich Nhat Hanh, a Vietnamese monk (who would never refer to mindfulness this way—that's my invention). Hanh counsels us to be fully aware during the most menial moments of our day. He often advises us to "wash the dishes when we wash the dishes." He means notice all the sensations that occur during this task: the heat of the water, the slipperiness of the glasses, the smell of the dish soap, the clatter of the plates as they are stacked, etc. This is in order to keep our mind focused on the task instead of what will happen later or what occurred before. But it also reminds us that the small things in our lives are beautiful and have purpose. Instead of rushing through them as burdens and chores, we can celebrate and appreciate them. This can help us alleviate feelings of resentment and build gratitude—in other words, put our perspective in balance.

This is, by no means, a comprehensive list of how to practice mindfulness. There is a world of information, ideas, and techniques out there, if you want to explore further. But, in the meantime, give these a try and see what works for you.

# Mindfulness and Removing Obstacles

In defining Kindfulness, I promised that greater awareness would help remove the mental blocks that keep you from achieving your goals. Mindfulness is the path to that awareness. Slowing the mind down long enough to identify your thoughts, and noticing the shifts in your body, are the first steps toward identifying the feelings behind them. To illustrate, let's go back to that car ride when we sped along for miles in mental blackout, and apply mindfulness instead of letting our minds drift endlessly. As soon as our thoughts begin to wander away from the road, we can take the opportunity to simply observe what is happening by asking and answering simple questions. For example:

**Q:** What am I thinking about?

**A:** Oh, I'm thinking about the conversation with my boss.

**Q:** Why am I thinking about that conversation?

**A:** I guess I'm worried about that conversation.

**Q:** Why am I worried?

**A:** I feel that she may have judged me harshly for handing in the project late. I sensed she was disappointed and possibly annoyed and didn't understand the reasons for the delay.

**Q:** Do I know this for sure?

**A:** No.

**Q:** Could there be other explanations for my fears and worries? Did I do something to bring them on?

**A:** I delayed starting the project because I was intimidated, and I spent too much time on it because I wanted it to be really polished.

**Q:** What can I do about it?

**A:** Ask for a chance to explain myself. Clear the air.

**Q:** Can I do anything about it now?

**A:** No.

**Q:** Will worrying about it change anything?

**A:** No.

**Q:** Am I OK right now?

**A:** Yes.

Having had this inner dialogue, we learn a few really important things:

1. We may have imagined the issue.

2. Our procrastination and perfectionism were obstacles to achieving what we wanted.

3. Everything is OK in the present moment.

And since we don't know and can't control what others think about us, we dismiss the thought until we can take an action to correct it.

Then we can get our minds back to reality. We can take a visual scan of our surroundings: asphalt, trees, road signs, other cars, a mailbox, a sunset, and so on. We also can take notice of the feel of the steering wheel in our hands, the gas pedal under our foot, the seat below our thighs. We can breathe in and smell any smells. Now we are mindful, in the moment, and less apt to act out with destructive behavior like overeating, spending, or indulging in alcohol or drugs when we arrive safely at our destination.

Speaking of eating, let's also return to my story at the beginning of this chapter about that cake. As I mentioned, my ongoing health goal is to maintain a healthy weight and eat nutritious foods. Gobbling cake when I am full would—over time—lead to weight gain. In the short term, it would probably cause me gastric distress and disappointment. When you face a moment of decision like I did, and if you have trained yourself well to slow down before you act, to pause and observe, you can ask yourself questions like these:

- Am I hungry?
- Why do I want it?
- Is it a reward or something to soothe me?
- If so, why do I seek a reward/soothing?
- Am I bored? Lonely? Resentful?
- How will I feel after eating this cake?

Later, we can use other tools like journaling or talking to a friend or trusted counsel to give us a clearer picture of how this scenario may repeat itself in our lives and lead to bigger problems.

Over time, this is how mindfulness becomes an invaluable tool to identify complex emotions and arrest patterns of destructive behaviors. When we practice this on a regular basis it becomes a kind of shorthand. We may not need to even go through all the questions and answers, because we can immediately identify what we're feeling and what our part is in it.

But in order to be able to summon up the strength to address these obstacles, we need to have a healthy ego and the capacity to forgive ourselves. That is why in the next chapters we will work to understand and cultivate the second component of Kindfulness.

# 3

# THE SELF-COMPASSION QUANDARY

*"Be patient with everyone, but above all with yourself*
*. . . do not be disappointed by your imperfections, but*
*always rise up with fresh courage."*

—St. Francis de Sales

## Why Are We So Mean to Ourselves?

When I read that quote, I wanted to know more about this St. Francis de Sales. And when I read that he lived in the 16th century as the Bishop of Geneva, I realized something very important: All of us, everywhere, throughout time, have struggled with self-compassion.

That being said, I feel that we are living in the harshest environment and period of history as far as self-compassion is concerned. Despite the expansive array of books, endless talk shows, and self-help gurus dedicated to making us feel good about who we are, most of mainstream popular culture sends a very different message.

Our movie heroes—especially male superheroes—are heralded for their self-sacrifice. They live alone and are deeply misunderstood. They often go without sleep and continue to fight badly wounded. Giving up to save themselves is never an option. The blame for failure to succeed in any mission always rests squarely on their shoulders. And they are surely never allowed one minute of pride and satisfaction—that's for lesser men.

Female role models in the media are perhaps even worse. They constantly tell us that we should have it all: the meaningful career, a satisfying and secure love life, an enviable home, healthy kids, a fit body, smooth skin, nice hair, financial security, and an exciting social life. And if we are missing any of these components, it is our fault. Worse, if we strive too hard to have all of this, we are also at fault for not seeking balance. We can't win.

And the evidence that these subtle—and not to subtle—messages are affecting us is everywhere. For example, nearly one-third of Americans report problems with sleep. While some of this is due to medical conditions, the fact is that millions of busy adults—especially parents and other caretakers—don't make enough time for sleep. If you think that this is acceptable, that just proves my point that our society devalues self-compassion.

That's because a poor night's sleep means more than just slogging through the next day. Long-term sleep deprivation (less than six hours a night regularly) can harm your health. In fact, sleep deprivation is linked to obesity, high blood pressure, poor concentration, and mood disorders. It also leaves us very little energy for doing the things that would show compassion and care towards ourselves, like exercising, healthy eating, and leisure activities.

It's not just sleep, of course. Our lack of self-compassion is evident in the rampant use of illegal drugs, smoking, unsafe sex, and other self-destructive habits. We choose to partake in activities that give us a momentary feeling of comfort—instead of actual support or care.

Perhaps more insidious, lack of self-compassion is most evident in caretakers. Our culture often makes them feel that they have no option but to put their children, parents, job, or community before themselves. They focus all their compassion on others and none on themselves. And we do little or nothing to arrest this damaging behavior. No, instead we celebrate it. We often watch human interest pieces on the local news about the single mother who works three jobs so that her kids have Christmas gifts, or the nurse who works night shifts so she can take care of her mother with Alzheimer's during day, and so on. While we can admire their kindness, generosity, and dedication to the people around them, in the long run they are hurting themselves.

Not only do these caretakers leave themselves little time for sleep, proper nutrition, or any kind of enjoyment, they put off going to see the doctor, a therapist, or the dentist. While not fun, these are actually important acts of self-love. So, like the superhero described above, their self-sacrifice leaves them wounded and lonely and vulnerable to bitterness, depression, and disease.

Why is hurting oneself in the name of caring for others not only acceptable but lauded?

It's not exactly clear, but today we are learning more about it. In her groundbreaking research and invaluable book "Self-Compassion," Kristin Neff explores the many reasons we—as a society—seem to value a blatant lack of self-compassion.

For one thing, living in a culture that values independence over community and cooperation—as is in the norm in the Western world—if we fail, we have only ourselves to blame. And often we take the blame with no understanding of our limitations, extenuating circumstances, or compassion. We believe it is solely a result of our defects of character—sloth, stupidity, imprudence, impulsiveness, and so on.

But she goes on to explain that how we are raised also greatly influences our tendency to be hard on ourselves. When parents use overly harsh words in a well-meaning attempt to keep their children from harm—e.g., "Stop playing with those matches. Are you stupid?!" or "Stop being so lazy and get to school. Do you want to get expelled?"—it teaches children two very dangerous things: One, berating language is a valuable motivational tool, and two, they are lazy or stupid if they are less than perfect, if they let down their guard, if they are human.

In adulthood, these warnings turn into regular internal chastisement at the smallest transgression. We're all guilty of calling ourselves "worthless" when we spill a steaming hot mug of coffee, or "idiot" when we make a typo on an important document, or "crazy" when have tried something new and daring that didn't quite work out.

But this self-berating and critical thinking is also a defense mechanism—especially when it's used in public. Think about how many times you've prefaced a question in a big meeting with something like, "This is probably dumb, but..." While this may feel like protection against criticism, it actually works to prejudice your audience that whatever is to come next is probably dumb.

We debase ourselves in other ways, like saying, "I know these boots are ugly, but I just needed to be warm today," in order to try to illicit the opposite response from friends, or at least beat them to the punch. For some reason it just seems easier—or at least more familiar—to accept this criticism from ourselves.

Again, this language and behavior is so habitual that most of us are unaware when it's happening. I've actually stopped clients mid-sentence to point out how cruelly they were talking about themselves and they've completely denied it—and that's when it had just happened. When it comes to self-compassion we're in a big quandary—to say the least.

# Self-Compassion Confusion

Self-berating, self-destruction, and feeling overly responsible for the happiness or well-being of others are deeply ingrained in our culture.

A big part of the problem is that most of us are confused when it comes to the very concept of self-compassion.

In this section, I am going to provide some clarity about what is and is not self-compassion, how it differs from self-pity and self-indulgence (commonly used interchangeably, but inappropriately, with self-compassion), and how it leads to another "self" term: self-care.

## Self-Compassion

Compassion in its most basic definition is a feeling of deep sympathy and sorrow for another who is stricken by misfortune, accompanied by a strong desire to alleviate the pain. It starts with an awareness of the suffering followed by kindness, gentleness, and patience. Compassion isn't judgmental or critical.

Every person is compassionate in varying degrees. I would wager that most everyone seeing a loved one lying in a hospital bed ill and in pain would feel sadness, fear, and frustration and would want to do what they could to help. Not all people would have the same depth of feeling about a wounded animal, a mother struggling with a crying child on an airplane, or the fall of a disgraced politician. That's because not everyone can summon up empathy or caring for the same things. We might judge the actions of the mother and not understand the discomfort of the child; we might not see the humanity in the politician because of his blunder; we might not feel a connection with an animal.

Therefore, to practice self-compassion, we must accept that we will have shortcomings, we will make mistakes, and we will fall down now and then. We are no better or worse than any other person—including those we love. In other words, we must see, understand, and embrace our own humanity and worth. And we must have the desire to help ourselves because we want the best for ourselves. And to do so without judgment or harsh criticism.

That's why many of us can be very compassionate toward others but show little self-compassion. We find it difficult to be patient with ourselves or accept that we are just like everyone else who goes through difficult times.

Self-compassion is an attitude toward yourself. It's about practicing virtues like patience, tolerance, understanding, and forgiveness. It's also about abandoning perfectionism, the habit of comparing yourself to others, and negative self-talk. The ultimate goal is to accept yourself exactly as you are today.

## Self-Indulgence

Having that frosted doughnut, spending your last $20 bill on a pedicure. These are acts of self-indulgence. Basically, self-indulgence is giving in to desire and impulses and allowing yourself to have or do things that give you immediate pleasure—that make you, and you alone, feel better temporarily.

In our culture, self-indulgence is frequently seen as an adequate replacement for self-compassion and self-care. Perhaps it is our market-driven economy, but in our culture there is a message to buy, eat, drink, and take as a way to feel better. What's confusing is that making ourselves feel better in the moment is held up as somehow good for us, as if it represents self-compassion or self-care.

But it isn't the case. In fact, self-indulgence is like making a pact with the Devil. When we indulge, we obtain the object of our desire immediately—whether it's a scrumptious but fatty and sugary dessert, an expensive purchase, or the thrill of sex with a stranger. But there's usually a price to pay. It could be tangible like weight gain, financial insecurity, or disease. Or intangible like guilt, shame, anxiety, and disgust.

Even innocuous forms of self-indulgence like taking a bubble bath are no substitute for self-compassion or self-care because they don't make a lasting positive difference.

Think of it this way, if you were a parent and had the money to buy either nutritious food or candy—not both—for a child, which would you choose? Practicing self-indulgence instead of self-compassion is ignoring your needs as a human to give yourself brief moments of pleasure. It's candy over cauliflower time and time again.

## Self-Care

Madison Avenue tells us that self-care is all external and needs to be purchased. Remember the frazzled woman from the bath-soap ads of the 1970s exclaiming, "Calgon, take me away!" Almost every self-care article you read in magazines mentions the ubiquitous bubble bath. The truth is a sudsy soak can't replace a nutritious diet, regular exercise, adequate rest, ongoing stress management, and healthy relationships. Getting your nails done, a night of martinis with your buddies, an ice-cream sundae, or buying that shiny new object, whether it's a necklace or a Mustang, won't help really care for yourself either. This is pampering, not self-care. Let's go back to the child example again. Self-care is treating yourself like a child in your care and under your protection: tenderly, with love, and by giving yourself what you need to thrive including rest, nutrition, affection, joy, safety, knowledge, and love. What this looks like day to day will be different for every person depending on their age, background, strengths, abilities, time and financial constraints, and preferences. In Chapter 7 of this book, I lay out what I call the Five Pillars of Self-Care and provide suggestions on how to use them to live a healthy life going forward.

If you've been putting off going to see your doctor, therapist, or dentist, remember that these important acts of self-care—while not necessarily fun—are crucial to your wellbeing. It never feels good to know you're procrastinating on something important, and those bad feelings can lead to unhealthy habits. Instead choose to take care of yourself the way you'd take care of your child or your puppy: with understanding, tenderness, and the conviction that taking care of yourself is non-negotiable.

Self-care might not always provide the thrill or enjoyment that self-indulgence does. No one would equate the feeling of doing squats for the first time in a long time with eating an ice-cream cone or getting a massage. But self-care can be pleasurable. A nice long walk, quenching a thirst with crisp, clean water, waking up refreshed after a long sleep, eating a fresh piece of fruit can all be immensely satisfying. As you begin choosing self-care over self-indulgence, in fact, you may find that the fruit becomes more appealing than the cookie. Now, not to confuse things, but self-care could mean giving yourself an indulgence now and then as a reward for all the things you do for yourself. It certainly doesn't mean living like a monk or prisoner.

Self-care is an action, while self-compassion is an attitude. But in order to practice self-care on an ongoing basis, we first must practice self-compassion.

# The Importance of Self-Compassion

As I've mentioned previously, self-compassion is one of the keys to lasting, positive transformation. We can all attempt to change with an attitude of harsh self-criticism and judgment, and it may work for a while. But when the going gets tough, the tough usually aren't able to show enough compassion and care for themselves to go on.

But when we work to change and to adopt new healthy habits and lifestyles with compassion, we are doing it not because we are worthless or unacceptable, but because we want the best for ourselves. And when we encounter blocks, obstacles, difficulties, and challenges, we are kind, patient, and encouraging.

I'm not alone in this thinking. Kristin Neff notes that researchers also think self-compassionate people may be more aware of their own faults, have more courage, and be more motivated to persevere.

Many people might believe that practicing self-compassion means you'll take it too easy on yourself, and be less ambitious or successful. In fact, the opposite is true. Research has shown that people high in self-compassion tend to have higher standards, work harder, and take more personal responsibility for their actions, according to Neff.

I'll give you an example from my own life. Years ago, before I became a health coach, I worked for a huge social services agency in New York City. It was a great organization doing invaluable work, but the culture there was toxic. Employees came in early and stayed late every single day regardless of the workload. In fact, they spent hours debating the smallest issues and redoing unimportant tasks. Lunch hours were unheard of. Personal time and vacations were frowned upon. In fact, one executive returned to the office just two days after giving birth. Everyone was miserable. Not only that, they couldn't seem to grow or improve their services. But they didn't know any other way of doing business.

I was hired by a brilliant woman who had recently taken a leadership position there, and wanted to shake things up while bringing more humanity to the workplace. Unfortunately, she had to retire just six weeks after I was hired because of an injury. One of the old guard took over.

Under this new/old leadership, I didn't fit in. I came in at 9 a.m. and left at 5:30 p.m. or 6 p.m. if there was a crunch. I took a lunch hour to actually eat. But unlike my stressed-out coworkers, my department flourished. We were able to undertake new campaigns and launch new programs, all while increasing revenue and improving efficiency. But unfortunately, my example never caught on, there was a lot of pressure on me to extend my hours for no reason, and I decided to leave.

Without self-compassion, I would never have been able to take care of myself in that punishing atmosphere. My physical and emotional needs were taken care of so I could do my work with vigor and creativity. It's as simple as that. Self-compassion also gave me the courage to leave the toxic situation and move into the unknown. I feel great sympathy for those who stayed and wished I could've helped more. But I've learned that self-compassion can't be taught. It must be cultivated from within. Now that you know what self-compassion can do for you, you're probably wondering how to find more of it in your life. Take a nice deep breath, because I'm going to help you find your way.

# 4

# CULTIVATING
# SELF-COMPASSION

There's a great expression that I personally need to hear over and over again: "If you are going to beat yourself up, use a feather, not a stick."

It can take a lot of time and practice to cease the negative behaviors and thought patterns that block us from having compassion for ourselves. These are deeply ingrained and are so familiar that we aren't even aware we are doing them. It's truly a challenge to stop berating yourself when you can't find your keys, to learn that you don't need to apologize before you voice an opinion, to rest when you've run out of steam, to say no when you want to, and to have patience with your progress. Sometimes we have to settle for beating up ourselves more gently while we're on the road to a new, kinder self.

When it comes to self-compassion, none of us is going to achieve this ideal fully or be able to practice it every moment of every day. And I am certainly no exception. In fact, very early on in the process of writing this book I had a mini (well maybe not so mini!) meltdown. I had a freelance writing assignment deadline, I was behind in getting a revision of my outline to my peer coach (more about that invaluable person later), the holidays were coming and I hadn't wrapped any gifts or decorated my home, I had a doctor's appointment, and my dog decided this would be a good time to have tummy problems. It was only 10 a.m. and I had yelled and cried at least twice already.

Then I got a call from one of my angels. Hopefully, you have at least one person who knows exactly what to say to calm you down, show you love, and talk you off the ledge metaphorically. Well, I spilled my guts about everything that was happening to me and around me, and all this pressure I felt, and she said in loving but teasing way, "Oh, you are being so mean to my poor Karen, why don't you show yourself some compassion." I paused and smiled to myself as I said to my friend, "I will give you an early Christmas gift…I'm going to give you the biggest laugh you'll have all day." Then I told her that the topic of the book I was toiling over, sweating over, beating myself up about, was "self-compassion." As I predicted, howling laughter ensued on the other end of the line. I joined in.

But then I was grateful for this meltdown. I could use this example in these pages to illustrate that self-compassion must be practiced every day. It is not bestowed upon us like a title from the Queen. It is more like a muscle. We must use it, build it, exercise it every day or it will shrivel away and disappear.

Answering the phone in the middle of my tornado of a morning was an act of self-compassion. The tiny seed of it was there. I just had to slow down enough (become mindful) to let it grow so I could restart my day with less pressure, smaller expectations, and greater appreciation for myself.

After hanging up, I thought about the kind words of my friend and saw that I was being way too tough on myself. I was able to realize that the gifts and decorating were not important and would get done some day—just not that day. When my mind stopped spinning, I could also see that I wasn't really behind in my book goals, I just wasn't far ahead (which is my comfort zone). I told myself that I would be able to meet my freelance work deadline because I had done it a million times before with less time to do so. And I knew my husband was there to help with the dog.

I couldn't see any of that when I was in the meltdown. I felt alone, scared, failing, falling, and very frustrated with my lack of super powers!

By cultivating that seed of self-compassion, I was able not just to calm down and continue my day, but to do so with self-care. I could prepare a healthy lunch, drink enough water, take breaks from writing—not out of a sense of duty, not because I "should" or I "had to," but because I love myself and care about myself enough to do these things.

That's just one more example of how self-care starts with awareness and self-compassion.

But just how do we stop the negative voices, unreasonable expectations, harmful habits, and tendencies to put everyone else before our own needs?

Cultivating self-compassion is a different journey for everyone depending on their family background, personality, the lives they have led, even where they live—believe me, we have our own style of self-berating here in New York City!

That's why in my practice we take an individualized approach, watching for the most appropriate opportunities and exploring the most effective approaches. But because I am here for you as a book instead of face to face, I will describe the different methods that have been successful for my clients and for me.

I'm going to offer assignment suggestions after each section to make it a bit easier to get started. Feel free to take what works and leave the rest, but please give them all a try before dismissing any of the suggestions based on preconceived notions or doubt. Explore one or two methods and move on to new ones when you feel comfortable. If it feels helpful, ask a friend or partner to do this with you or just to provide support and accountability. (I'll cover more about this tool in Chapter 6.)

## Self-Soothing and Affirmations

Words have power.

Saying things out loud—whether to yourself or another person—has enormous power. From religious traditions of confession to modern-day psychotherapy, from moving speeches and theater to intimate relationships, we witness how voicing our innermost thoughts can provide freedom, motivation, acceptance, relief, support, and strength. Words also have the power to comfort and soothe. Just remember skinning our knees at the playground or having a bad day at school and hearing our mother's sympathetic voice. Or suffering our first heartbreak and being told, "It's their loss!" by our best friend.

But we can't always rely on another person to provide inspiration, comfort, and strength. No one can be with us all the time everywhere. This is when we must learn to rely on ourselves. And this is when self-soothing talk and affirmations become an invaluable tool.

Affirmations are simply positive, specific statements usually said in the present tense. They can help you to overcome self-sabotaging, negative thoughts, or visualize your goals and work toward positive changes to your life.

If you're rolling your eyes, you're probably a bit dubious about affirmations. Many of us associate them with less-than-credible, new age, pseudo psychology. Or perhaps you're of a certain age and recall the hilarious "Saturday Night Live" skit with Stuart Smalley, who would stare into the mirror in his pastel sweater and declare, "I'm good enough, I'm smart enough, and doggone it, people like me."

This is a good time to suspend any prejudices and be open to something whose efficacy is backed by both anecdotal successes and scientific evidence.

Proponents claim that, when practiced deliberately and regularly, affirmations reinforce a chemical pathway in the brain, making the connection between two neurons stronger, and therefore more likely to conduct the same message again. Thanks to some fascinating research, we know that self-affirmation can protect against the damaging effects of stress around academic performance and other important problem-solving situations. In another study, published in the Journal of American College Health, researchers found that women treated with cognitive behavioral techniques, including positive affirmations, experienced a decrease in depressive symptoms and negative thinking. The problem is, most of us feel vulnerable or just plain wacky talking to ourselves aloud. But consider this: Most of us do this all the time—just with the opposite intent and result.

Think about all the times you call yourself a less-than-flattering name (Idiot! Stupid! Jerk! Fool!) or exclaim to yourself, "What the $#% is wrong with me?" when you've committed a sin no greater than spilling your coffee or leaving your credit card at the restaurant. As I have explained, these insults to ourselves, repeated often, become believable and can seriously damage our self-esteem, confidence, pride, and motivation.

We don't think that speaking to ourselves brutally is odd or "new age-y," so why would we feel this way about saying kind things to ourselves aloud?

Even if you buy into this concept of affirmations without reservation, you might feel a bit awkward or be stumped at what to say during your first attempts. Here are some ideas:

- For confidence in relationships: I am lovable. I am beautiful. I am perfect just as I am. I am a catch!

- For confidence in work: I am knowledgeable. I am experienced and prepared. I am a valued employee with a lot to offer.

- For self-soothing in times of crisis or anxiety: I am fine right now. It's OK to be scared (worried, mad, sad, lonely). Everyone gets scared from time to time. I'm not alone. I am taken care of. I am surrounded by love. I have everything I need in this moment.

- For personal and health goals: I am getting stronger every day. I deserve to be healthy (prosperous, successful). I can do whatever I set my mind to. I am not afraid of hard work. I am creative. I am a leader.

- I am a force for good in the world.

I also believe that saying your name aloud before these phrases makes the affirmation more potent. Here's an example of what I said to myself after my mini-meltdown:

"It's OK, Karen, you had a bad morning, we all have bad mornings, but everything is actually OK. Just be good to yourself and take things a bit slower today. You'll be fine. You are fine, everything will get done, it always does."

## Assignment:

Try starting the day by saying one of the affirmations above (depending on your needs/goals) aloud—in a mirror for extra credit—and build up to saying it a few times a day. I would suggest finding a private spot, so you feel completely comfortable.

Still cynical and not ready to try? Then read on and try something else.

But in the meantime, I urge you to try becoming aware of any negative self-talk, and work to minimize or eliminate that. Then, if you find that you feel better once you've nipped that harmful habit, perhaps you will be persuaded to do the opposite and speak to yourself in gentle, kind, and supportive ways.

Couldn't hurt, right?

# Gratitude

Gratitude is the key to squashing the dangerous tendency toward self-pity experienced by many of us who feel we've not reached our expectations, been cheated in life, or haven't fulfilled our dreams and hopes.

For example, after years of trying to lose weight, be free of nagging aches and pains, sleep for a full night, it's common to slip into self-pity. In addition to the discomfort of carrying extra weight, being fatigued, and more, lingering health issues often separate us from others and lead to a feeling of isolation and depression. Which, of course, exacerbates the original issues. That's when self-pity arises and turns us inward in a negative way.

Self-pity tells us that we are unfortunate, alone, helpless, hopeless, doomed, jinxed, unwanted, damaged, unworthy, and so on. With gratitude, we realize that these beliefs are out of proportion or totally false. Gratitude shines a light on our assets and changes our perspective. In fact, in recent years, psychologists have studied the mental health benefits of gratitude, including greater levels of happiness and optimism in addition to increased alertness, enthusiasm, and goal-attainment.

Gratitude is a huge part of self-compassion because it allows us to see and feel the things in our lives that are good instead of focusing on what's not working, what's wrong with us, etc. When we realize that we are surrounded by good things, we can begin to understand that we are lovable, capable, and deserving of a good, healthy life.

According to University of California Davis psychology professor Robert Emmons, grateful people take better care of themselves and engage in more protective health behaviors like exercise, a healthy diet, and regular physical examinations. They also avoid self-destructive behaviors like smoking, excess drinking and drug use, or binge eating. In other words, they practice self-care.

But for many reasons, gratitude can be hard to summon up. It isn't necessarily something you're born with, and even if you acquire it, it can't just be switched on and off like a lamp.

Believe me, I tend to think of myself as a cynical New Yorker, not a Pollyanna. But I was tired of being cranky all the time—it wore me down and made self-care more challenging. When I'm in a grateful state of mind, it feels more like I'm floating down a gentle river than swimming against the tide.

So if I can do it, you can too! Here are some tried-and-true methods:

### 1. Write a Daily Gratitude List (also a great tool in mindfulness)

We all have something to be grateful for, but often don't feel that way. Sometimes it's big things like health and a place to live. But if we sit down to write a list, often times we can find the subtler things like being grateful for a husband who is as goofy as you are. (That's on my list.) Doing this every day or a few times a week helps more gratitude rise to the surface. It's even better when you involve friends. I know a group of great young women who share their list by text every morning—what a fabulous way to start the day! The first few times may feel awkward, but soon it will be second nature.

### 2. Say Thank You

Make it a practice to look people in the eye and say, "Thank you." When a stranger holds the door for you, don't just walk through or mutter, "Thanks," under your breath. Stop, smile, make eye contact, and say, "Thank you." It will give you an immediate rush of happiness. Be sure to do the same for the cashier in the grocery store (even if she doesn't return your gaze), your waiter, your coworkers, even your family. As with affirmations, voicing your thanks sends a powerful message to the brain that you are indeed grateful. Thinking it, or forgetting to even acknowledge it, doesn't.

## 3. Give Yourself Credit

Sometimes we don't realize how far we've come until something outside of us reminds us. Maybe you saw someone huff and puff as they climbed a long set of stairs and realized that you don't anymore, thanks to all the cardio you've been enduring. Or you helped a friend figure out her iPhone, which used to baffle you. But you don't have to wait for the external stimulus; instead, make sure you check in with yourself periodically regarding challenges and issues you've been facing and honor any progress—no matter how slight. And when you realize you've achieved something, give yourself a pat on the back. It could be a tangible reward like a weekend away or a new coat, but you could also announce it on social media, put it in your prayer or meditation, tell friends, write it in your journal, or just say out loud, "Good job!"

## 4. Honor Others

Surely there is someone in your life who has truly made a difference. Maybe it's a friend who was there for you at your lowest. Or a teacher who helped to shape your worldview. Or a formerly under-appreciated parent. Make sure they know it and do it in a memorable, meaningful way. Take them to a special lunch or, if the person is no longer alive, write them a beautiful letter and place it somewhere meaningful. You will feel a profound sense of wellbeing instantly. People who show gratitude and altruism find that it boosts their confidence, ego, and sense of compassion for themselves.

### Assignment:

Pick one of the options above to try at least once this week. If it feels meaningful, keep it up. If not, move on to another.

# Forgiveness

What on earth could forgiveness have to do with self-compassion and self-care?

Well, let's see if this scenario sounds familiar. You're trying to stick to a diet on a day when your boss is nitpicking, or your mother pushes your buttons, or you learn that some of your friends went to dinner without inviting you. What happens when you get home alone and you're feeling lonely, angry, sad, or resentful? If you're like many of us, you get a case of the "F--- it's." You ditch your good eating intentions and down an entire package of chips, or order in pizza and eat until you are more than full, or indulge in cake and candy even though it doesn't give you pleasure. And that's just how you treat yourself after a small injustice.

Then there are deeper hurts. Perhaps you've never forgiven your father for leaving the family, can't seem to abandon the resentment of being fired from your first job, or still hurt from being rejected by the object of your affection. When we carry these wounds around for months, years, and decades they erode our entire outlook, often leading to patterns of destructive behaviors.

Ironically, when we feel hurt we sometimes inflict more pain and suffering on ourselves. We may know consciously that others hurt us, but we just can't seem to forgive ourselves for the situation and we abandon self-compassion. This leads us to indulge in overeating, using drugs, overspending, and so on. And as the years go by, we get more and more disappointed at the state of our lives and health and that just makes us spiral down even further.

## Daisy's Story

Daisy found herself in this awful cycle. She came to me because she wanted to live healthier and lose weight. She was full of energy, spirit, and resolve at first, but when I'd ask about how she did between our sessions, she would apologize for not being able to complete the small suggestions we agreed on like walking to work, or cooking one dinner at home instead of picking up Chinese takeout or pizza. She couldn't look me in the eye and would berate herself for being stupid and lazy.

I knew, deep down, Daisy wanted to help herself, but there was something big stopping her. So I encouraged her to be gentle and kind to herself and open up about what was going with her on a deeper level. We talked and talked about her frustration with her career, among other issues. She had once been an aspiring singer and her future looked bright. She was even chosen to perform a duet with a world-renowned recording artist. But this "big break" never panned out and she blamed herself. She also held grudges against family and friends whom she felt betrayed her, and she felt like a fool for letting it happen.

She had little to no compassion for herself, no forgiveness for the mistakes, disappointments, and perceived failures that are just part of life. I knew that this was a huge obstacle in her path to finding the love and courage to coax herself into the initial uncomfortable steps towards healthier living.

So, we began to talk about forgiveness—for others, for sure, but mostly for herself.

Letting go of her past was the key to a huge shift in attitude for Daisy. After a while, her tendency to berate herself diminished and was replaced with gentle encouragement. Soon, she no longer wanted to eat a candy bar on the way home from work, stay up all night binge-watching TV, and subsist on junk food. She also grew more grateful for her current job, she started exercising in the morning, and began to cook—and truly enjoy—most of her own meals. This began a positive cycle of pride and self-esteem leading to weight loss, an enormous reduction in joint pain, and an improved social life.

The thing is, none of us can control what others do, nor can we erase the hurts of the past. The only thing we can control is our reaction to it. If we can forgive, we can move on. We can make a conscious choice to let go of anger, resentments, vengeance, and other emotions that eat away at us, upset us, and cause us to act badly.

It's not about letting someone off the hook for a wrongdoing, or forgetting about the past, or forgetting about the pain. And it certainly does not mean that you stick around for future maltreatment from a boss, partner, parent, or friend. It is about setting yourself free so that you can move forward in your own life.

The key is understanding the humanity in all of us—that we are all capable of making mistakes, acting out of pain and confusion, and being less than perfect. I have a friend who says that when you want to be more understanding of someone's unkind action or thoughtless remark, just picture them in a hospital gown, because we are all sick in one way or another.

If we realize we are all human, all flawed or struggling, we can learn to be more forgiving of ourselves—which is often more difficult than forgiving others. Multiple studies—including a recent one at Johns Hopkins University—have shown that forgiveness transforms anger and hurt into healing and peace, and can help you overcome feelings of depression, anxiety, and rage, as well as personal and relational conflicts.

Of course, even for the most enlightened among us, forgiving isn't easy. It takes a leap of faith and some patience. I've found these steps can help:

## 1. Share Your Story

Talk to sympathetic friends and family about the offending incident and your desire to forgive. Many times, we are ashamed of our anger or feel vulnerable recounting a hurtful incident. But if we can find the courage to open up to another human being, we can find comfort and often times a totally new perspective on the issue. Old wounds usually become warped, twisted, and grossly out of proportion, haunting us without real reason. Talking it out releases the ghosts and monsters from your brain and makes the situation right-sized.

## 2. Reverse Roles

This can be difficult, but try to see the situation from the other person's perspective. Imagine how they felt, what was going on for them in the moment, what fears or misconceptions they may have harbored. If you know their history, you might develop compassion for the hurts that they may have endured in life that led them to hurt others. Let's take the example of the nitpicking boss. If you've ever been a boss, you might recall enormous pressure to be responsible for your work and the work of those you supervise. Once you see it from this perspective you can see the action wasn't a personal attack and is forgivable.

## 3. See Your Part

Sometimes our willingness to hold grudges comes from the fear of admitting our role in the offense or misunderstanding. It doesn't mean we are fully responsible, guilty, wrong, or bad. Going back to the work example, if you rushed to finish a project for fear of missing a deadline or because you just wanted it out of the way, perhaps you weren't as careful about mistakes. Maybe this has happened before. It doesn't mean you are a bad worker or a bad person, it just means you need to tamp down impulsiveness and be a bit more prudent when it comes to your work. We all have room to grow. Once you accept this, then forgiveness of yourself and others can flow more freely.

## 4. Take Control

Being angry is a choice. It doesn't feel like it most of the time, but it is. Don't let holding a grudge keep you from feeling free, open, and powerful in your own life. Holding on to a resentment is like taking poison and waiting for the other person to die. Knowing that you are hurting yourself makes the choice to forgive easier (not easy). You can use affirmations to help you give up anger and forgive by repeating, "I am not angry, I forgive, I am at peace no matter the situation."

## 5. Forgive Yourself

Perhaps most important, when all the above is said and done, forgive yourself for holding on to the resentment, for being unclear or confused, for any part you've played.

## Assignments:

1. Ask yourself if you are holding an old resentment: Is this resentment "taking up space" in your head, affecting your emotions, worrying you, or causing guilt or pain? If so, ask a friend to try to help you use the steps above on it.

Or...

2. Use these tools to forgive yourself for something you can't seem to let go of. Maybe it's gaining weight over the years, messing up an assignment at work, hurting a friend's feelings. Whatever it is, if it's getting in the way, let it go. Get clear on the situation, understand your history, and see yourself as human and beautifully imperfect like the rest of us.

# Lighten the Load

It's an unfortunate irony that the folks who seem to offer the most compassion, care, generosity, and kindness toward others are often the ones who are the hardest, cruelest, least giving, and most demanding of themselves.

Of course, I've told you my story of working full-time, tending to my husband and dog, doing volunteer work, keeping a tidy home, paying bills, all while dealing with a dying mother-in-law and father at the same time. The last person I thought of was myself. I neglected my health and most of my emotional needs for a long time and it took its toll on my body, mind, and spirit.

That's why, in my practice today, I try specifically to help caretakers. I find that many people in their 40s and 50s—women, especially—are overwhelmed trying to meet the needs of their children and ailing parents, along with all their other responsibilities. And, believe me, most of them continue to hold enormous expectations for advancement in their careers, for being social, for having an attractive home, etc. After doling out so much care and compassion to others, there is nothing left for them. Nothing.

These wonder women pose a difficult challenge because they feel righteous in their choices. How could anyone abandon a child or parent in need? What I try to help them to understand is that I am not suggesting abandoning any important responsibility. For them, it's more about setting priorities, jettisoning certain obligations, and lowering standards and expectations enough to give themselves a break—in other words, practicing self-compassion so they can practice the basics of self-care.

The first step is "lightening the load." This can mean different things to different people. For some it will mean giving up smaller duties and roles (like PTA volunteer or book club president), or asking to work from home or take a leave of absence.

But the most important aspect involves asking for help and relying on others. If this made you pause, gasp, or shudder, this section is especially for you.

Many of us cringe at the word "dependent" and prefer to accomplish things on our own. It just seems easier to have a sense of total control. But it comes at a high cost. Not only do we leave ourselves little time or energy for self-care, we often grow resentful toward others for not pitching in.

That's the obvious stuff. By not asking for help and support, we also miss out on human connection, new information, and the feeling that we matter to our loved ones. I'll give you a very small example of how asking for help—how practicing "interdependence"—helps:

Before the mass popularity of selfie sticks, Yelp, GPS, and Google, tourists would stop Rollo (my faithful Border collie companion) and me on the street to ask for directions, to take their picture, or for a recommendation for the best pizza in the neighborhood. We would happily pause to assist them and often gave them more than what they were looking for. Sure, you can go take that water taxi for a quick ride but the Staten Island Ferry is free. Yes, you can see the Statue of Liberty in this shot, but it's better around that bend. And since my old neighborhood didn't have very good pizza, I'd suggest a short scenic stroll to Chinatown for some authentic Szechuan instead.

It saddens me to think that tourists would now rather stare at a five-inch screen than ask a New Yorker for advice. They are missing out on a real human interaction and the knowledge, humor, and encouragement it might include. And this is just one example of the downside of not asking for help.

There's a lot more at stake when we choose to rely on ourselves too much. In fact, lightening the load, lowering our expectations of ourselves, and freeing up time is absolutely essential to becoming a fully functioning, happy, well adjusted, and healthy adult.

I know for many of you it will still be hard to switch gears from independence to interdependence. So aside from cultivating self-compassion, here are a few reasons why you'll benefit from asking for help.

## You'll Help the Helper

You may be shy about asking for help because you don't want to be a "burden." But think about it: If you've ever helped anyone with anything, you know it can make you feel really good. Why rob someone of that great feeling?

## You Won't Miss Growth Opportunities

From holding "tree pose" in yoga to figuring out Excel charts, from making your first loaf of bread to doing your taxes, sometimes we need the advice or know-how of a more experienced person. All the YouTube videos, apps, and manuals you can find are never going to take the place of the one-on-one, hands-on assistance of a living breathing human being. Think back on all your great learning moments—I bet none of them happened in front of a machine.

## You'll Combat Loneliness, Depression, Stress, and Illness

When we ask for help we build connections—whether it's from friends, acquaintances, or business associates. This fosters a sense of community, which protects us from feeling alienated, anxious, and depressed. Loneliness and mood disorders often lead to self-neglect and illness.

## It Strengthens Your Character

You may be the most generous person in the world, but giving help when you've asked for it yourself allows you to develop a greater sense of empathy for those in difficult situations. And while we're taught to have pride in being self-sufficient, it's less a moral strength than a blessing of talents and good fortune mixed in with some stubbornness and arrogance at times. Understanding our weaknesses and shortcomings, and our commonality with others, promotes humility—which is a virtue.

## It Prevents Burnout

If you get sick or injured or just too fatigued to move, who will help your loved one or do your work? If you allow others to help lighten the load, you will fend off burnout and have more energy—not just for others, but for yourself. It's the opposite of a vicious cycle.

Most of all, accepting help builds self-compassion. Like building any muscle, each time we do it is strengthening the message that we are worthy of help.

And here's something I know will make it easier. In order to lighten the load, you don't always have to gather volunteers from friends and family. You can hire people. As a friend always says, "Just throw money at the problem!" If your budget allows, you can hire babysitters, gardeners, and a multitude of professionals to take part of the load—and with no guilt.

You can also order groceries online, buy pre-chopped vegetables, have your laundry picked up, and other "luxuries" of modern life that cost a little more but save you precious time.

Finally, a big part of lightening the load is not adding to the load. That means learning to say no. This was a tough one for me—as it is for so many others who hate to disappoint friends, coworkers, and family, and like being a superhero. But why say yes and then feel burdened or resentful? Think of it this way: your true friends don't want you to agree to an evening out, a favor, or any other request if it makes you overwhelmed, overburdened, and stressed-out. They will understand if you reply with a simple, "No, thanks."

The first time I did this (I used my oldest friend as a guinea pig) was one of the most liberating experiences I've ever had.

The first step in letting go of this sense of responsibility and control is being willing and then finding that kernel of self-compassion that says you're worth it. We all have it deep down. Just try to find yours and cultivate its growth.

## Assignment:

Review the following list—or brainstorm your own list—of common responsibilities and duties. Pick one and try to eliminate it entirely, pay to have it done, or delegate it to a friend or family member.

- Housekeeping
- Grocery shopping
- Cooking
- Dishes
- Snow shoveling
- Bill paying
- Laundry
- Gardening
- Dog walking
- Taxes
- Home repair
- Projects at your job
- Child care
- Senior care
- Shuttling family to appointments
- Clubs and organizations
- Volunteer work
- Birthday parties and other hosting responsibilities

# Get to Know Yourself

Everyone knows this famous line, delivered by Polonius in "Hamlet": "This above all: to thine own self be true…"

You might also remember that "Hamlet" is a tragedy, and one of the reasons nearly every character comes to a gruesome end is that Hamlet is unable to be true to himself. He seeks endless counsel and advice, hems and haws because he can't seem to access or act on any genuine feeling. And everyone basically dies because of it.

OK, this may be an extreme version of what can happen when we aren't true to ourselves, I'll admit. But hopefully it caught your attention. Because learning to know yourself, accept yourself, trust your own judgment, and act in your own best interest is a huge part of self-compassion and ultimately self-care.

Too many of us have shut down our natural personalities in order to fit in, please others, and be accepted in all situations. Instead of being ourselves, we become a chameleon of sorts. Decades into this charade, we may be totally unaware of our true desires and preferences. When this happens, it's nearly impossible to fully practice self-compassion and give ourselves the things and experiences that provide satisfaction and joy. It's like trying to buy a gift for a perfect stranger.

## Beth's Story

I'm reminded of Beth, a smart, ambitious young woman who came to me because of her heightened stress and chronic insomnia. Beth grew up as one of six children of busy, successful parents. From an early age she had to share toys, clothes, space, and parental attention with her siblings. Instead of standing out, she just got lost in the shuffle, tried to stay out of the way, and learned that it was easier to appease everyone else.

When we started working together, I was amazed that she seemed to have absolutely no opinions about her exercise regimen or favorite foods. She ate a bland sandwich every day for lunch because she thought that was what lunch was. In the beginning it was like pulling teeth to get her to talk about herself. But, we kept at it. After a while we learned that she did, in fact, love cycling, because she could identify that her mood was better on the days she was able to go for a long ride. Trying some new, healthier lunches, we learned that she got more pleasure from grain bowls with lots of interesting ingredients—some of which she thought she'd hate (probably because her siblings hated them).

Once she got accustomed to sharing her preferences and opinions about tangible things like food and exercise, a new part of her opened. She began talk more freely and fully about her life. Together we learned more about what specific things caused her to worry and which relationships gave her peace. These crucial bits of info helped us devise a plan that allowed her to sleep more soundly and manage stress.

The lesson is that getting to know yourself honestly and profoundly—like getting to know a new romantic partner or friend—takes time and a bit of effort. But the payoff is huge!

Since I can't be there to gently coax you to open up and explore your feelings and tastes, here are some practices that will help you get to know yourself better:

- Write in a daily journal. Note what made you happy, scared, mad, etc.

- Spend quiet time alone.

- Go to movies, museums, and other cultural activities alone and take note of what you liked.

- Meditate.

- Try different cuisines and recipes; sample new fruits and vegetables.

- Read the newspaper and notice what you feel (angry, encouraged) after different stories.

- Make lists—lots of lists! For example: your best attributes (generous, funny, hard-worker), things you could improve about yourself (judgmental, impatient, procrastinator).

- Write your life story.

- Start a blog.

If you are already aware of certain preferences and interests, focus on developing them. In other words, let your freak flag fly! Whether you have an affinity for quilting, secretly binge-watch old episodes of "Northern Exposure," love polka music, or make your own sausages, don't be afraid to share these passions and peculiarities, because they're what make you you. When people truly know you and accept you, you are one step closer to accepting yourself and practicing self-compassion and Kindfulness.

Speaking of acceptance, being true to yourself also means learning to love yourself exactly how you are today. This can be difficult if you want to change your body or your habits. But the two can coexist. Until you can embrace yourself entirely, take time to appreciate the wonderful and unique things you do like about yourself: your brains, humor, freckles, bright eyes, smoky voice, great laugh, compassion, puzzle-solving abilities, communications skills, organizational acumen—whatever it may be. Make a list, say it in the mirror, or write a poem to yourself about it. Just make sure that you let yourself know how great you are every single day.

This will also mean being good to yourself and treating yourself to a reward now and then. In Chapter 6, we will talk about the tool of rewards. Without doing this work, we aren't able to reward ourselves, because we don't know what makes us happy. And rewards are a potent motivator in self-care. So this is yet another reason to get to know yourself.

Now, about what not to do. The number one restriction is comparing. When we don't know ourselves well, we'll often look to others as examples or to tell us what we "should" be doing or wanting to do. This will just lead you down the wrong path.

For example, volunteering may fill another person with joy and purpose and leave you feeling flat or drained. Some may think that dancing isn't exercise, but for you it may light your inner fire. So even if you're not the most graceful dancer, do it. The more time you spend focusing on yourself, and listening to your intuition, the clearer your purpose(s) will become. And the more you express your gifts, talents, and passions, the more you will feel self-compassion.

Another don't: Don't exaggerate or brag. Be proud of exactly who you are, your level of skills, education, strength, etc. You don't need to tell tall tales to make up for insecurities or perceived shortcomings. When we lie about our accomplishments and talents, we send a dangerous message to our brains that we aren't enough—that there's something wrong with us. This, of course, is the opposite of self-compassion.

Finally, being true to ourselves also involves being reliable and trustworthy. Self-reliant people arrive on time, finish their work, and fulfill their promises—especially to themselves! People who don't trust their own judgment and doubt their opinions and choices are those who rarely keep their word to themselves. That means if you join a gym, go to the gym. If you say you're going to get more sleep, then shut off the TV and go to bed at a decent hour. If the check-engine light is flashing, take your car in ASAP. After all, who admires and wants to follow a leader who is undependable? I also suggest that you make an extra effort to keep any promises you make to yourself and show up on time. Make a decision and stick to it.

Not every decision needs to work out perfectly, but staying true to our choices strengthens the muscle of self-confidence, which leads to great self-compassion.

## Assignment:

Try something new. Go to a class you've never taken at the gym, sign up for an adult education course, ask your boss if you can take on a new set of responsibilities, learn chess (that's on my list) or a new language, go skydiving or rock climbing, sing karaoke, take a cooking class.

Or, if you can't find something you like yet, start making lists of all your likes and dislikes in categories like music, TV, food, clothes, animals, nature, exercise, and so on to get to learn what you'd like to try.

# Spirituality

I sometimes hesitate to talk about spirituality because it can conjure up all kinds of images, from crystals and vortices to ghosts and angels, from fringe cults and TV evangelists to the friendly church on the corner. And—depending on your experiences and point of view—any of these could be a major turnoff.

But really, spirituality is what you make it. It's whatever is beyond you, whether that means connections to other people, a kinship with nature, an understanding of a higher power, a devotion to a deity—or something else that I haven't conceived of but you have!

The reason I do take the risk of raising this issue is that connection to a higher power or higher purpose allows many of us to feel loved, seen, and cared for. And if we feel worthy of care and protection, then we can learn to practice it—self-compassion and Kindfulness—on ourselves.

Again, this isn't just my opinion. This is backed by serious research. In fact, many studies have shown that a full and robust spiritual life often provides a sense of joy, commitment, and inner peace. And people who have a regular spiritual practice usually report having a more positive outlook on life, according to a 2007 survey by sociologists at the University of Wisconsin, Madison.

It makes sense. When you feel a part of the universe, you do what you can to stay alive and vibrant. All of a sudden the next set of crunches, swapping a burger for a salad, improving your mind, and getting to bed at a decent hour just comes more naturally.

In contrast, those who isolate from others, shy away from finding meaning and purpose to their existences, and cut themselves off from the grandeur of the universe tend to feel helpless, hopeless, anxious, or empty. It is hard to care for yourself—eat right, exercise, sleep well, and avoid toxic habits and people—if you feel like that.

If you're interested in building or boosting your spiritual life, you may choose to return to the religion of your childhood, deepen an existing practice, or explore ones you are unfamiliar with. Just see what feels right and what doesn't work. Or if you just want to feel more peace and develop a deeper sense of wellbeing, all you need to do is carve out some time for solitude and quiet.

Here are some suggestions to get started:

**Go Out in Nature**

Even if the ocean, mountains, and forests don't immediately inspire holy feelings for you, spending time in the great outdoors puts our individual existence in perspective. Viewing the amazing chasm of the Grand Canyon carved from millions of years of nature's forces is a completely different experience than looking around a room filled with things you bought and placed there. If a trip of this scale is not in the cards, just try to find a local spot where you can't easily view any man-made structures. Make this a habit.

**Meditate**

Sit and focus on your breath or try a walking meditation, chanting, or a yoga or martial arts class to see what works best for you.

### Listen to Music

Many people find an enormous spiritual feeling listening to their favorite symphony or rock ballad. Music has a way of opening our hearts and eliciting feelings we often tamp down.

### Read Spiritual Works

Pick up a book on a religious tradition you know little about, or just a volume of inspirational essays from people like Oprah, Martin Luther King, Gandhi, the Dalai Lama, the Pope, or others.

Whatever you choose, the goal is to get out of yourself and feel connected to something greater than you. And hopefully, that feeling will inspire greater self-compassion.

## Assignment:

1. Ask yourself where and when you feel most at peace. Try to recreate this feeling.

Or...

2. Explore a new and unfamiliar spiritual practice that interests you by visiting a house of worship or reading up on the traditions.

# Fun

Part of being a good parent is having fun with your children. I was lucky enough to be raised by the most fun mom on the block—so I know this to be true. She made up games, challenged us to create silly songs and poems with her, read to us, took us ice-skating and to watch the Mets, let us turn our apartment into one large, kid-filled tent, and so much more that I could write an entire book about it.

She made us—my sister and me—feel special and loved. And these games and excursions were also much-needed distractions from the more challenging parts of our childhood, which included an absentee father and living close to poverty. Along with feeding us, clothing us, and keeping a roof over our heads, keeping fun in our lives was essential to how my mother cared for us and let us know we were loved.

That's true of most kids, but as adults we tend to diminish the importance of fun. We become all work and no play. I'm here to tell you that all work and no play slowly kills our spirit. And when our spirits are low, we aren't very nice to ourselves.

That's why including fun in our lives as adults is an important factor in Kindfulness. Furthermore, if that fun involves something healthy (which I hope it does!) like sports, learning to cook, movement, and freeing ourselves from isolation, it becomes a valuable part of a self-care plan.

Just look at the healthiest people you know, athletes at the top of their game, people running in the park—they look pretty happy and they seem to enjoy life. Maybe happy people like to stay active or maybe active people are happier? Who knows? But either way, it's worth a try. According to the mental and emotional health website HelpGuide.org, in addition to boosting your self-compassion, fun has been proven to:

- Reduce stress
- Calm the mind
- Strengthen your heart
- Increase energy
- Improve memory and concentration
- Build stronger relationships

- Promote sounder sleep
- Help recover from loss and grief

You might be saying to yourself, "I have fun, I don't need to read on." But I invite you to ask yourself just how—and how often—real, joyous fun happens in your life. When you answer, don't include watching Netflix or curling up with a good book at the end of the day—that's relaxing and maybe even intellectually satisfying but it isn't what I'd call fun. Not for the sake of this part of self-compassion and self-care.

Fun involves laughter, a freeing sense of adventure, silliness, lightness, and childishness. It is the kind of activity where the time zips by and you wish you didn't have to stop. I'm lucky enough to feel this on a daily basis with my beloved pup, Rollo. He makes me chase him and hide under the covers at least twice a day inside, and have multiple adventures outdoors—squirrels beware!

But in addition to those small daily doses of fun, I try to schedule a real fun outing at least once a month or so. For me these include getting dressed up to watch an awards show, cooking a big batch of chili and watching a sporting event with friends, hiking in the woods or spending time at the beach, seeing live music performed, playing miniature golf, and even watching "Jeopardy" over the phone with a competitive friend of mine.

## Assignments:

1. Schedule one of these activities or come up with an idea of your own:

   - Riding a rollercoaster
   - Karaoke
   - Haunted house tour
   - Kayaking, canoeing, or pedal boating
   - Skiing or snowboarding

- Ice-skating
- Hosting a costume party
- Hosting a game night
- Playing touch football in the park
- Going out dancing
- Taking a class in painting, cooking, fencing, or pottery
- Trivia night at a local pub
- Seeing an interactive performance or play
- Going to open mic night
- Appearing in open mic night
- Smash room (pay money to break things safely – a favorite of one of my clients!)
- Taking a belly dancing class

If your idea of fun isn't listed here, or you're stuck in a rut and out of ideas, pick up a local magazine like "Time Out" for inspiration.

2. Be open to taking spontaneous "fun" breaks throughout the day.

# Finally...

# Spreading Compassion

It is a beautiful cycle: The more love we offer out, the more love we feel toward ourselves. No one ever felt good about themselves after reaming out a slow sales clerk. But we often feel pretty proud and self-content when we do an anonymous good deed like helping a lost tourist or giving a banana to a hungry street person.

When you're feeling down, make a concerted effort to reach out and be extra kind—you'll see dividends pay out in self-love immediately. Take to heart these timeless lyrics from the Beatles: "...and in the end, the love you take is equal to the love you make."

Now, armed with self-compassion, you are ready to greet the more common obstacles that block people from achieving their health and life goals.

# 5

## GREET YOUR OBSTACLES!

*"Obstacles are like wild animals. They are cowards but they will bluff you if they can. If they see you are afraid of them... they are liable to spring upon you; but if you look them squarely in the eye, they will slink out of sight."*

—Orison Swett Marden

If weight loss—or any change of habit—were simple and straightforward, we'd all be slim and healthy, right? We all know, sadly, it isn't. In fact, any major change we seek is usually fraught with complications and obstacles.

Our minds and bodies get used to a certain way of living—even if it no longer serves us. We crave the familiar because it feels safe, and change feels wrong. So we throw up obstacles to change without even knowing it.

There are many obstacles that are obvious and easy to detect. For example, many of us struggle with finding time to take the steps involved with leading a healthier life, such as working out, cooking at home, going back to school, etc.

And then there's money. Joining a gym, buying organic vegetables, paying for classes, all require an increase in spending.

But honestly, those obstacles—probably the most frequently used excuses for not changing—are the easy ones. They are the most fixable. Why? Because we can see them. It's obstacles that we have yet to identify that truly hold us back.

You and I both know that we can find time and money for the things we want that are easy and instantly pleasurable (in most cases). More than that, there are ways to exercise, learn, and eat healthy that don't need a bump in your budget. And there are ways to better manage your schedule to fit in time for all these things as well.

## Then What Are the Real Obstacles?

Well, they vary from person to person. And the way to find them is with a little digging and nice amounts of candor, willingness, and courage. I have found that these strengths can be summoned up once somebody is desperate enough for change. When years of frustration and disappointment mount up, and when all the excuses are gone, then we can mine for the truth.

If you don't have the gift of desperation, it may be difficult to find the willingness, courage, and candor to analyze your thoughts and behavior and to do the work ahead. I would ask you at this juncture to take a good look at your life and see if it matches with your expectations. Are you as healthy, fit, and strong as you thought you'd be? Do you have the energy you want? Do you get the sound sleep your body deserves? Do you feel serene instead of anxious or agitated most of the time? Are you satisfied with your work and relationships? If the answer to any of these is no, then ask yourself this most important question: Do I deserve something better?

Of course you do. But if you couldn't feel a resounding "YES," you may be experiencing two of the thorniest obstacles that prevent people from even seeking help: complacency and denial.

In my story, I related how I was under the false perception that weight gain, sluggishness, digestive issues, and achiness were just part of living once you hit the ripe old age of 40. Hah! I wouldn't have said I was happy with my state of being, if you had asked, but I didn't know enough to be unhappy either. I was complacent. Because my career as a fundraiser didn't require bodily strength, feeling achy and weak didn't affect my income or status. And because my husband was basically blinded by love to the changes in my appearance (a blessing and curse), I didn't experience any emotional consequences of my weight gain either. I just kept buying bigger-sized clothing, or opting for stretchy, comfy clothes. And I made that classic assumption that my stuff had shrunk in the closet mysteriously over the season. The gain was subtle and insidious enough to make it believable—because I wanted to believe it. That about sums up both complacency and denial.

In psychological terms, this is considered the "precontemplative" stage of the widely accepted "Six Stages of Change," developed by Prochaska and DiClemente in the late 1970s to understand addiction.

The six stages of this model are:

1. Precontemplation
2. Contemplation
3. Determination

4. Action

5. Maintenance

6. Termination

Individuals in the precontemplation stage of change are not even thinking about changing their behavior. They may not see it as a problem, or they think that others who point out the problem are exaggerating. In the next phase, contemplation, people are willing to consider the possibility that they have a problem, and the possibility offers hope for change.

According to this model, there are many reasons to be in precontemplation—but in my opinion, it comes down to complacency and denial. Most folks in that stage do not seek my help, so I cannot offer them coaching, support, and assistance to move past it. My job is to coach clients who are ready to make changes—changes that they choose, when they choose them. And, I would venture to guess that, as a reader of this book, you have gotten past precontemplation, and that is why you are interested in learning about a new solution to transform your life.

But there are cases when a person would seek help even if they are in a precontemplation stage. For example, they may be aware that they feel sick and tired but can't see the cause.

This is where Kindfulness can help. Through mindfulness and cultivating self-compassion, they may come to a new realization that an overwhelming job, troublesome relationship, or destructive habit like overspending is causing stress that leads to overeating, improper sleep, and other behaviors that leave them feeling sick and tired.

There's another, less common, aspect to the precontemplation stage, and that is hopelessness and self-hate. Some people think—whether it's in the way back of their mind or front and center—but don't often say, that they don't believe they deserve to be healthy. To me, that's the saddest statement a person can make. We all deserve to be the healthiest version of ourselves. No matter our past mistakes, our current responsibilities, lifestyles, and obligations, no matter what others say, we have the right to feel good and live without unnecessary pain, fatigue, fogginess, sluggishness, extra weight, or whatever ails us. Having been introduced to precontemplation, you may be thinking of someone you know who is in this stage. Don't let their current complacency or denial prevent you from giving them a copy of this book. (But keep your own! You'll want to refer back to it often.)

And for those of you ready for change...

Now, take a deep breath and join me as we greet your obstacles. You don't even need that much courage. They shouldn't really scare you since you know them already in some way. That is why I use the term "greet." We want to approach this as a positive opportunity to learn what has been holding us back. We all have developed quirks and defenses that no longer serve us. They are part of us, and therefore shouldn't be despised or feared. Our job now is to identify them, greet them with patience and understanding, and then to dismiss them with love, like a thought during meditation. To help you identify your obstacles, in these next sections I'll describe the most common obstacles experienced by my clients and me, and how you can use greater awareness and mindfulness to move them aside and live a stronger, healthier, more satisfying life.

If you feel a twinge of guilt or shame, a wave of anxiety, or a sudden burst of memories and thoughts, chances are that you identify with that obstacle. Great! That means you are well on your way to moving it aside and reaching your goals. Just make sure you are kind and gentle to yourself in the process.

# Obstacles: Boredom and Lack of Purpose

"Idle hands are the devil's workshop." I'm not one to usually quote the Bible, but this is a favorite saying of mine. That's because I've seen time and time again that boredom can be the worst offender when it comes to derailing us from our health goals, and that is why it comes first in these descriptions of obstacles.

Even the busiest among us gets bored from time to time. It's usually at the end of the night. We kick back on the couch, put on the TV, and lounge for a few well-deserved hours. We're often alone, and we aren't distracted by deadlines or demands from other people. It's just us and our thoughts. And that's when the trouble starts.

If we're trying to quit smoking, the cigarettes start calling to us. If we are seeking to break off a troublesome relationship, this is the time we feel compelled to text or call that person even though we know it means complications and entanglements. If we are trying to manage stress, our thoughts begin to swirl and circle and grow large and out of proportion. Whatever your bad habit is, boredom is like adding Miracle-Gro to it.

I know. During the day, I go from a project to a meeting to yoga to walking the dog and I often need to stop myself to eat something. But when my responsibilities are over and the night stretches out in front of me—and I stretch out in front of the TV—I begin to obsess about dessert. And after dessert, I begin to think about salty snacks like popcorn. My stomach is full, my nutrition is complete, but I think I want more food. That is the effect of boredom. We are uncomfortable with the lack of activity and purpose and seek an emotional impact (pleasure) from something—in this case, food.

Before you can break free from the cycle, you must be able to distinguish between squashing the boredom trigger—the obstacle—and legitimate physical needs. This can be trickier than it sounds. But there are clues that can help you discern your physical and emotional needs. I will use the food example:

Boredom hunger comes on suddenly and strong. It hits you in an instant and feels overwhelming and urgent. Physical hunger, on the other hand, comes on more gradually.

Boredom hunger craves specific comfort foods. When you're physically hungry, almost anything sounds good—including healthy stuff like salad and fruit. But emotional hunger craves fatty foods or sugary snacks that provide an instant rush. You feel like you need cheesecake or pizza, and nothing else will do.

Boredom hunger often leads to mindless eating. Before you know it, you've eaten a whole bag of chips or an entire pint of ice cream without really paying attention or fully enjoying it. When you're eating in response to physical hunger, you're typically more aware of what you're doing.

Boredom hunger isn't satisfied once you're full. You keep wanting more and more, often eating until you're uncomfortably stuffed. Physical hunger, on the other hand, doesn't need to be stuffed. You feel satisfied when your stomach is full. That's because emotional hunger isn't located in the stomach. Rather than a growling belly, you feel your hunger as a craving you can't get out of your head. You're focused on specific textures, tastes, and smells.

Boredom hunger often leads to regret, guilt, or shame. When you eat to satisfy physical hunger, you're unlikely to feel guilty or ashamed because you're simply giving your body what it needs. If you feel guilty after you eat, it's likely because you know deep down that you're not eating for nutritional reasons.

As I said, boredom can happen to any of us from time to time, or at a certain point of the day. But for many, like my client Nina, boredom is a symptom of a larger, more pervasive issue: lack of purpose.

## Nina's Story

Nina is a vibrant, intelligent woman in her early 60s. When we began our health coaching sessions, her grown daughters had recently returned home to join the family business. Nina took this a cue to retire from the business and finally relax. But she noticed that she was putting on weight in addition to experiencing other health problems. She couldn't sleep through the night and was plagued with worry. The first thing she admitted to me was her love of sweets and that she couldn't stop snacking.

Because we met at her home, it was easy to make my first suggestion. I looked around and there was tasty food everywhere in sight: cookies, breads, candies, freshly baked muffins, etc. Nina loved to cook and entertain, and she wanted to be ready to host at any instant. But having all this temptation in sight was making her resolve to stop snacking nearly impossible.

By our second session, all the treats were out of sight and bowls of lovely fruit had taken their place. Nina reported that her snacking was better...well, on some days. There were still days and times when she couldn't control her urges, nor find the resolve to have a healthy breakfast (another goal). The more we talked, the more we began to realize that Nina's days were too empty. She missed the hustle and bustle of work, but not the stress and fatigue. So, we worked on a plan for her to be more social, more engaged and busy, and agreed on some simple steps to get there, including language lessons, museum tours, exercise classes, long walks with friends, and other ideas for activities.

Nina was like a different person at our next session. She could barely contain her enthusiasm and gratitude. Over the previous weekend she had hosted some old friends at her home—five or six people, including young children. Most people would've been exhausted, but Nina was refreshed. More important, she was proud to tell me that not only was she able to resist snacking, she hadn't even thought of sweets—even when they were everywhere.

This success strengthened her commitment to our plan and she was able to lose weight and—with the additional help of some breathing exercises—lessen her anxiety and sleep better.

The fact of the matter is that human beings need a purpose and connection. It is part of our evolutionary make-up. And when we lack this purpose and connection, the body and mind know that something is out of whack and we do what we can to quell this feeling.

While so many of us overly busy people dream of retirement, vacation, or even just a night to ourselves, we must be careful to make sure we feel connected and engaged. This doesn't mean treating ourselves like work horses who never stop and never have a moment to rest—no, that creates problems of its own.

## How to Greet this Obstacle

Use mindfulness to watch for signs of boredom/lack of purpose. In addition, these questions will help. Remember, please don't judge your responses.

- Do you find that TV makes you want to eat or smoke or drink more?

- Do you go shopping even when you don't need new clothes or other items?

- Do you find yourself staring in to the fridge or pantry between meals looking for something you'd like to eat?

- Do you often eat dessert even when you're full?

- Have you started a bad habit after leaving a job/retiring?

- Do you sleep poorly after quiet or un-busy days?

- Do you feel depressed or agitated on the weekends or after work?

- Is it hard for you to take a vacation because you don't like downtime?
- Do you eat/drink/smoke or engage in other unhealthy behaviors more when you're alone?
- Have you gained weight since your children went off to school or you lost a job?

## How to Apply a Kindful Solution

The first step in breaking this cycle is to determine whether you're eating—or doing any self-destructive behavior—out of boredom or you are actually hungry. If you answered yes to one or more of the questions above, I would suggest starting with some affirmations and gentle soothing talk using these phrases as an example:

- My stomach is full/my needs are taken care of.
- I don't need this bag of chips, new handbag, etc.
- I can put this activity off for a day.
- I can do something healthy instead.
- I will feel better resisting this urge.
- My long-term health goals are more important than my short-term desire.
- I deserve to be healthy.

The next step is finding ways to stay relaxed but engaged and find alternatives to food (sex, shopping, drugs, etc.) that you can turn to for emotional fulfillment. Here are a few Kindful solutions that have worked:

### Connect

Call someone who always makes you feel better, play with your pet, or look at a favorite photo or cherished memento. Even writing an email or liking a friend's post may make you feel more connected. But avoid social media if it tends to trigger envy or other negative feelings.

**Move**

If boredom has made you anxious, expend your nervous energy by dancing to your favorite song, squeezing a stress ball, taking a brisk walk, or keeping busy (see below).

**Soothe**

If you're bored but exhausted, treat yourself with a hot cup of tea, take a bath, light some scented candles, wrap yourself in a warm blanket, or just go to sleep (if you can).

**Stimulate**

If you're intellectually bored, read a good book, play computer games, explore the outdoors, indulge in a hobby (knitting, playing the guitar, scrapbooking), or do some work (sorting out drawers, job-related assignments, or homework). Don't do this last suggestion if you feel it may increase anxiety.

# Obstacles: Prejudice/Arrogance/Judgment

The eye-roll. Looking away. The scowl. A loud humph or sigh. Silence. I can always tell when a client is less than thrilled with a suggestion I make. It's understandable to react negatively to things that we've tried in the past and didn't like, but to have that kind of reaction to something new and unfamiliar isn't beneficial. This attitude is referred to as "contempt prior to investigation" in self-improvement circles. We're all guilty of it. No one walks around with a completely open mind. But when you are trying to break old patterns and live a better, more positive, healthier life, trying new things comes with the territory. I remember visiting a friend years ago who had been into Eastern spirituality and new-age practices for a while. Let's just say, I was not. And when I awoke at 6 a.m. (well before my preferred waking time) to the sound of her chanting, I said to myself, "That, I will never do!" and

I put the pillow over my ears and attempted to go back to sleep.

Well, don't you know, five years later, at a yoga retreat, I was taught to meditate through chanting and something clicked. My mind was clear and calmer that it had ever been. Ah, I thought, never say never. Of course, I was happy to have found this new tool, but it's a bit sad that I could've been benefiting from it for five years if I had just had an open mind. But my arrogance and judgment got in the way.

We aren't born with arrogance and judgment, we come by them naturally as we go through life. They are ways of controlling our environment, protecting ourselves from the unknown, keeping us from getting hurt. As with all personality issues, they arise from fear (which we'll talk more about later in this chapter). And the stronger the personality we have, the more deeply they are ingrained.

Often times, to feel more confident with ourselves, we use judgment and arrogance as protective armor. We make our identities more black and white because gray areas are scary. Macho athletes who want to maintain their air of masculinity are loathe to take up ballet as a way to improve flexibility and balance; meat-and-potato eaters hold on to prejudices against kale and quinoa; and hard-driving, hard-working, type-A personalities are offended by the suggestion of an afternoon nap.

My job is to gently nudge and to find ways to make these suggestions palatable while my clients keep their dignity and autonomy. Often this means cutting through common excuses, which are just arrogance and judgment wrapped in a neat package.

Take these three common excuses for example:

### *"I won't exercise."/"I hate exercise."*

Usually this will come from someone who was scarred emotionally in gym class or thinks of exercise as drudgery. Having come from a family who got their cardio shopping, I understand. I hate the word exercise.

It sounds like exorcism. But I like yoga. I look forward to walking with my dog along the river. I love hiking. I enjoy swimming and kayaking (and almost anything in the water). And I got a real kick out of boxing in my younger days. Movement is natural. It makes our bodies feel good and our moods even better. That's why I know there's some sort of physical activity for every single person in the entire world; I just have to help clients do a bit of exploring to find what works for them.

### "I can't meditate because my mind just wanders."

The truth is that every human being with brain waves and a heartbeat will have a wandering mind while meditating. That's the point. Meditation is the practice of trying to still the "monkey brain." And no one—with the possible exception of the Buddha—has ever achieved a perfectly still mind during meditation. People who offer this excuse are usually afraid—on some level—of slowing down long enough to really hear their own thoughts. Or just afraid of failing (see fears). But there are many who associate meditation with a certain new-age/hippie type of person, a gentle open soul. This prejudgment is a way of protecting themselves against what others might think of them if they were to attempt this enormously helpful practice. At this point, I explain all the types of meditation, from simple breath work and counting (which usually seem the least "granola-y" and are therefore more acceptable) to chanting, guided meditations, and more. If I can get someone to count their breaths for two minutes during a stressful situation, usually they come back for more.

### "I don't need to log my food."

Sure, nobody looks forward to taking time to learn an app or keep track on paper of what they are eating. Again, it sounds like drudgery. But we take the time to learn apps we like and keep other lists and do other hard work, right? When people object to logging food it's usually because they believe they already know what they eat (arrogance) and that this seemingly simple tool couldn't help (arrogance and judgment.) What I like to explain about food logging is that it's like cleaning out a closet. Sure, you put all the stuff in there so you ought to know what's coming out, but we always forget a few dozen items stashed in the back, or just how many photo albums we have, and how crowded and dusty the shelves have become. In other words, we may have an idea, but not a completely clear picture, of the nature and size of the inventory. It's the same for logging food. We remember we had eggs and toast for breakfast, but when we write it down we see we had three eggs cooked in butter and two pieces of toast with butter and jam. And we didn't even consider the juice and coffee with half-and-half. At the end of the day, instead of having a vague understanding of the food, we see all the calories, fat, sugar, and other components of our meals, and are apt to catch some things we might have overlooked entirely. Logging food also makes us practice mindfulness. Knowing we will have to record each meal forces us to pay attention to what we're eating. And, guess what, that often means we make better choices.

Avoiding the unfamiliar—especially when it can improve our lives—is not only sad, but it can be harmful. While for many of us losing weight would help us look better in our clothes and have more energy, for others it is a life or death proposition. Poor dietary habits and obesity are risk factors for diabetes, heart disease, and Alzheimer's, just to name a few life-threatening conditions.

## How to Greet this Obstacle

We all judge, but if we continually judge out of fear and misconception— without any evidence or prior knowledge—then this becomes an obstacle. Practicing ongoing mindfulness is most useful in greeting this obstacle, noticing both our physical (eye-rolling, sighing, rigidity) and emotional (discomfort, awkwardness, fear, judgment) reactions to new ideas or unfamiliar suggestions. Consider the following questions:

- Do you often decline invitations to new types of experiences?
- Do you dismiss suggestions from friends on books to read or things to try?

- Do you often ignore doctors' advice?

- Do you stick to the same recipes and food choices?

- Are you cynical about alternative approaches to health?

- Have you rejected trying meditation or a spiritual approach to managing stress?

- Do you doubt what you can't prove?

- Do you believe that others are watching your behavior and judging you?

- Would you call yourself "risk-averse" with your money and investments?

- Is it important that your friends and family share the same opinions and ideas as you?

If you answered yes to two or more of these questions, prejudice and judgment are probably obstacles for you.


## How to Apply a Kindful Solution

As always, start with mindfulness. Each time you recoil at a suggestion that could promote greater health, or at trying a new kind of food, exercise, stress management technique, sleep suggestion, whatever, check your motives. Ask what image it conjures up. See if that image provokes fear, repulsion, or a sense of ridicule. Then you can dismiss those thoughts and fears because they are no longer useful to you.

Then you can ask yourself kindly, with patience and understanding: What have I got to lose, and what do I have to gain? When the scoreboard shows that "gain" is the winner (which it always does!), then you can breathe and ask yourself to summon up the courage and willingness to try it.

You can ease fear and awkwardness by asking a friend to try something new with you. Or you can survey friends on social media to see if any of them have tried whatever is new. You may find their positive responses and encouragement enough to go for it. Remember to reward yourself whenever you do overcome an old fear or judgment.

# Obstacles: Loneliness/Isolation

When you share an apartment with a husband and 60-pound Border collie in one of the busiest cities on the planet, it's hard to feel alone. But that doesn't mean that I—and millions of others—don't experience loneliness. It's not about physically being alone, it's more about feeling disconnected to other human beings. In fact, I believe the most painful kind of loneliness is feeling apart while surrounded by people.

A Brigham Young University report on the subject describes it as an "ever-present, self-perpetuating condition that pushes people away from relationships that sustain us and make us happy." Even worse, this emotional state can increase the risk for mental and physical health issues. This study even showed that the increased mortality risk of social isolation is comparable to that of smoking, and that loneliness is about twice as dangerous as obesity. In fact, loneliness profoundly impacts physical health in a variety of ways, potentially contributing to:

- Depression
- Headaches
- High blood pressure
- Insomnia
- Heart Disease
- Fatigue
- Chronic Pain

Humans—whether we like it or not—are social animals. Our need to love, be loved, and be part of something larger than ourselves is written in our genetic code; it's a survival instinct. When we ignore this essential part of life, we suffer. That's why relationships are just as important as the food we eat, sleep, exercise, and other primary components of good health.

As an obstacle to getting healthier, loneliness will often make us hold on to habits that no longer serve us, such as endless TV watching, working longer than necessary, staying out late, and even more insidious behaviors. My client Fred did all these things.

### Fred's Story

Fred is an ambitious, highly successful, and gregarious man in his early 50s. He makes friends wherever he goes, learns difficult systems in a snap, and seems to turn everything he touches to gold. But Fred had chronic insomnia. He'd have trouble falling asleep, and often wake up in the middle of the night and be unable to go back to sleep. He was operating on little sleep for months and he was frustrated and disturbed when he asked for my help.

For sleep issues, I do an extensive inventory of a person's home environment in addition to their eating, drinking, and exercise habits and other pertinent lifestyle behaviors. When this exhaustive study was completed I was astonished. Fred was doing a dozen or more things to sabotage his ability to get a proper night's sleep. He lived on a busy street but kept the window open, which allowed noise and streetlights to invade his bedroom. He kept the door to his bedroom open even though his roommate often came home late at night and made a racket. He drank copious amounts of coffee. He ate and drank right before bed. He stayed out late frequently on work nights. And he watched TV in the bedroom and kept the phone on next to his bed.

When I pointed out these behaviors he was rigidly unwilling to change even one. Months of disrupted sleep, fogginess, and fatigue wouldn't sway him to make a single change. So I began to ask questions: Why do you want to hear noises? Why do you go to the bar almost every night? And so on. Fred didn't come out and say he was lonely, but he could admit that he felt comforted by the sounds and presence of other people. After much encouraging, I got Fred to agree to cover his electronics, quit coffee after 3 p.m., and cut off food and drink by 10 p.m. More important, I suggested a few things to combat loneliness that wouldn't interfere with getting a good night's sleep, like seeing and talking to friends on the phone earlier in the day, keeping photos of loved ones by his bed, envisioning his favorite people in his mind and saying goodnight to them one by one as he went to sleep, keeping a gratitude journal, and more.

For Fred, this is an ongoing process. When he is able to adhere to these suggestions, he does sleep better. But until he can feel a deeper human connection and feel taken care of and safe, his body will continue to awaken him.

## How to Greet this Obstacle

No one wants to admit they're lonely. But the fact is, we all are from time to time. Sometimes, we've suffered a loss or moved to a new place. Other times, it's a sense of isolation that comes from feeling like you're different. And then there are those who just can't seem to find deeper connections, because they were traumatized by past relationships or family issues. There is no shame in feeling lonely. And most people will not judge you and will want to help, if you reach out. If you think you may be lonely, but aren't sure if it is affecting you, be mindful of your life. Perhaps write in a journal or do a reality check.

Consider these questions:

- Do you feel uncomfortable/antsy if your partner or roommate is away?

- Are you unable to fall asleep in an empty home?

- Do you keep electronics on constantly?

- Do you fall asleep with the TV on?

- Do you scroll through social media more than one hour a day?

- Do you delay bedtime to talk on the phone, watch TV?

- Do you stay out late on work nights or school nights so you can be with others?

- Do you eat, drink, use drugs, shop more when you're alone?

- Have you ever stayed in a bad relationship for fear of being alone?

- Do you only cook when it's for someone else?

## How to Apply a Kindful Solution

If you answered yes to two or more of these, your loneliness may be an obstacle to reaching your goals, and you would be served by trying some effective Kindful solutions.

It is also important to know that the feeling of loneliness has little to do with how many people are around you, and you are not to blame. Practicing forgiveness, as outlined in the "Cultivating Self-Compassion" chapter, can be very helpful.

Loneliness often goes hand in hand with vulnerability and low self-esteem, which deter many people from taking action because they feel stuck living this way or they are afraid of rejection. The first step to alleviating loneliness is accepting that you have the power to change it. Thankfully there are plenty of ways to conquer loneliness and cultivate good healthy relationships once you find the willingness to take action. Here are a few strategies that can help:

### Focus on Quality Over Quantity

You just need a few people to depend on and who can depend on you.

Identify friends you love and trust and make the effort to reach out to them often. Take a risk and open up to those you live or work with to foster a sense of intimacy in your current relationships.

## Say Yes

If you spend too much time alone, accept invitations to parties and outings, and sign up for classes and workshops, no matter how unmotivated or awkward you may feel (most of that is anticipation anyway). Promise yourself to stay an hour, and if it sucks, go home. Keeping this promise will boost your self-esteem and you might just have fun. I should know…saying yes to a workshop I was hesitant to attend is how I met my husband!

## Volunteer

Giving your time to a cause you believe in fosters a sense of altruism, which can lead to greater happiness, gratitude, and life satisfaction—plus you might meet some like-minded people and forge a new friendship.

## Adopt an Animal Companion

There's a long list of health benefits associated with spending time with animals, including improved mood, lower blood pressure, and decreased stress. Sharing your life with a pet can also lead to more exercise and social interaction. But please consider your time and physical and financial limitations before choosing a pet. Dogs don't thrive on long stretches of time alone and need exercise and discipline. But cats like alone time, and smaller animals like guinea pigs are cheaper to care for but can still cuddle.

## Seek Help

If you believe that chronic depression or social anxiety is at the root of your loneliness or if you suffer with trauma from past relationships that makes it difficult for you to get close to people now, please find a therapist you trust to help you.

**Limit Social Media**

While sites like Facebook and Instagram seemingly keep us connected to others at all times, they can actually make matters worse. A recent study of Facebook users conducted by the University of Pittsburgh School of Medicine found that the amount of time they spent on the social network was inversely related to how happy they felt throughout the day—mainly due to envy of other people's perceived lives and activities.

## You are Not Alone

Remember, even if you feel alone, you are not alone. More often than not, there are friends and family who love and care about you just waiting for you to reach out. Further, it may be comforting to realize that you are part of the human race, full of people who feel doubts, fears, and loneliness—just like you—from time to time. Cultivating a spiritual outlook, as described in the previous chapter, may help you.

# Obstacle: Perfectionism

I remember a client protesting, "I couldn't be a perfectionist, I'm far from perfect." There's much confusion about the meaning of perfectionism. Instead of being ideal, it's measuring everything and everyone—especially yourself—against an ideal standard. It's seeing the glass as not only half-empty but too small, too streaky, and not expensive enough. A perfectionist will spend the day cleaning and scrubbing because she can't rest until the house is entirely clean. Of course, because a house will never be entirely clean and in perfect repair, she will never be able to fully rest or be satisfied.

This is an intolerable state of being that leads to added stress and anxiety, and often causes people to engage in self-destructive behaviors like overeating, drinking, smoking, overspending, etc. Ironically, even though these behaviors aren't ideal, they give people a sense of control. And control is what's missing for people who seek, but will never achieve, perfection.

Perfectionism is also an obstacle to taking steps toward leading a healthier life. For example, many of us believe that starting a weight loss journey—or any health improvement—will be so monumental that the stars must align before beginning. So we put it off until we have oodles of time (which will never happen), or we have lots of excess money (which we don't need), or we complete a big project so we can devote our full attention to it (again, impossible).

Of course, like the person who cleans before the house cleaner comes, many of us want to get in better shape before we attempt to join a gym or lose weight. It sounds insane, but this is the torturous thinking that goes along with perfectionism.

And then there are those like Kim, a dedicated and eager client, who will want to find the perfect plan and gather all the tools to execute before taking action.

## Kim's Story

Kim is a delightful and dynamic woman in her mid-30s who had struggled to maintain a healthy weight, was often stressed out and anxious, and had trouble finding satisfaction in work and in relationships. In addition to these issues, Kim had been diagnosed with Candida overgrowth, a difficult to treat fungal condition that is often the result of a diet including too much sugar. When she received the diagnosis, she was bound and determined to do something about it. But she was resistant to cutting back on sugar. Instead, she spent weeks researching Candida cleanses that required drastic lifestyle changes, severe dietary restrictions, a course of exotic and expensive herbal remedies, and learning complicated recipes. She bought books and signed up for online courses, but had trouble pulling the trigger and starting any of the plans. How could she know which course of action was the right one...the perfect one?

She was in a tizzy to say the least. During all this analysis and weighing and decision-making, she was still carrying around extra weight, still suffering from the symptoms of Candida, still achy and fatigued, plus now she was confused and frustrated. That's when we decided that we would try just one aspect of the one of the plans for two weeks and see how that worked. We started by eliminating foods with added sugar—tough enough for anyone to accomplish, but for Kim it had the definable boundaries that allowed her to envision completion and success.

From there we moved on to limiting other forms of sugar, trying one herb at a time, and incorporating other suggestions that came highly recommended from Candida specialists. Within weeks, Kim began to see that the Candida was a blessing in disguise because it forced her to limit the sugar that was the main culprit of her excess weight and joint aches. After her Candida subsided, she was able to add back in fruits and other foods with naturally occurring sugars. And she no longer craved the sweets she originally felt she couldn't live without.

Perfectionists will often delay attempts to get healthier or try everything at once. That's why they need to break their goals down to smaller, more attainable, and—most important—concrete steps with measurable outcomes. For them, deadlines work as motivation and provide the structure that actually makes them more comfortable.

For example, instead of vague advice like "start exercising," perfectionists are better served by a goal of walking for 30 minutes a day, five days a week. Instead of "eat less," perfectionists are more comfortable with the suggestion to cut out 300 calories a day from their diet. And so on. Perfectionists can also tend to put off any changes because they know innately that it will not bring them satisfaction or happiness. I remember spending a grueling two weeks painting my old apartment and did a marvelous job as an amateur. But I couldn't see it. I sat night after night when I should have been winding down and watching TV, noticing flaws and jumping up to repaint spot after spot. This went on for months. My husband even mentioned it during our marriage vows!

Years later, when I wanted to repaint, this torturous scenario came back to me and I just refused to even get started.

When I see this situation arise in clients, it often comes in the form of not wanting to try yoga because they won't be as advanced as the other students, or not wanting to cook at home because they just can't get the recipe exactly right. Or, commonly, they feel that others will judge them, whether it's in the gym, at home, or at work, for not doing whatever course of action perfectly.

## How to Greet this Obstacle

Remember, perfectionism doesn't mean that you, or your life, are perfect. It's focusing on flaws and shortcomings instead of the whole picture. And it's stopping before you start because you are worried you won't be able to accomplish something perfectly. Most people may realize they are a bit negative or critical but shy away from calling themselves perfectionists. You don't need to use this label on yourself to see if perfectionist tendencies are harming you.

Even before applying mindfulness to watch for these tendencies, take a moment to forgive yourself for this attitude, which you probably acquired over years as a way to protect yourself. Then, take four or five long cleansing breaths and consider these questions:

- Do you have trouble starting projects?
- Once you start a chore or project are you able to stop halfway through?

- Have you avoided learning a new skill or taking a class because you fear you won't excel at it?

- Do you work extra hours or late into the night to complete or polish a project?

- Do you apologize for your work even when others deem it satisfactory or excellent?

- Do you question major purchases or choices weeks, months, and years after the fact?

- Are you unable to find satisfaction in finished projects?

- Do you berate yourself for minor mistakes such as losing keys or saying the wrong name?

- Do you often try to do everything at once?

- Do you do work for others because you fear they won't get it "right"?

## How to Apply a Kindful Solution

If you answered yes to two or more of these, then work on mindfulness to recognize when your tendencies arise and block you. You could also try breaking down large goals into smaller ones, doing reality checks, and more to find patience, acceptance, and perspective.

You can also use soothing talk and affirmations such as these:

- My thoughts are just thoughts.

- I am strong enough to accept any outcome.

- Nothing will stop me from enjoying life or getting healthier.

- What are the positive aspects of my choice or project? Do they outweigh the negative?

- I am OK today just as I am.

- It's natural to make mistakes.

- People love me because of my flaws; they are what make me, me.

- None of this will matter in five years.
- We all have to start as beginners.

For my clients and me, it's understanding that the world won't end if you fall on your face doing crow in yoga (which happened to me). Just put down a blanket first to soften the blow.

# Obstacle: Procrastination

We all procrastinate from time to time—it's human nature. We put off chores, dawdle away a whole working day, or leave important tasks to the last minute and rush to complete them. But procrastination—even for a brief amount of time—can take its toll.

When we linger in bed for "five more minutes" before getting up, we are usually not feeling free or relaxed. Instead, we are often scolding ourselves in our heads. Or when we put off an intimidating project at work, we watch the clock, seeing the day progressing without anything to show for it. We worry about tomorrow and the next day knowing that responsibilities will continue to pile up. In other words, in even short periods of procrastination, we start a flow of toxic stress and anxiety.

Imagine when that goes on for days or worse. Well, we don't have to imagine because over the years, psychologists have found that procrastination can affect your health. Here's how it works:

1. Putting off important tasks can result in stress as you rush to meet a deadline at work, miss paying bills, disappoint friends or colleagues, or are surrounded by clutter and mess.

2. Stress, in turn, is related to various illnesses ranging from headaches, flu, backaches, and digestive issues, to conditions like heart disease, high blood pressure, acute anxiety, and depression.

3. Procrastinators also tend to have a poor self-image and are harder on themselves, which contributes to elevated stress levels.

4. Because of low self-esteem and stress, chronic procrastinators often turn to drugs and alcohol, food, smoking, and other self-destructive behaviors as coping tools to deal with stress and to disengage from reality.

5. Stress also negatively affects the duration and quality of sleep. And fatigue crushes motivation, which leads to more procrastination... and the cycle continues.

## Why then Would Anyone Procrastinate?

Well, there are as many reasons as there are personality types. For example, some need the rush of excitement that comes with finishing something off at the last minute. These folks can seemingly only operate under pressure and enjoy the thrill that comes with completing a task under the wire. They just don't realize the toll it's taking on their nerves and wellbeing.

Others put off things due to a fear of failure (see upcoming section). Then there are people who procrastinate because they simply can't make a decision—that's often related to perfectionism, as was described previously.

We also tend to put off doing things when we have poor self-discipline. People who have relied on doting parents, or overly caretaking spouses or partners, will often feel less responsible for themselves and, therefore, less inclined to tackle anything challenging or unpleasant. They expect that someone will swoop in at the last minute to save them.

Of course, many of us will delay anything that is painful, boring, awkward, or just generally disagreeable—like a dentist visit, an apology, filing taxes, cleaning the toilet, etc. And finally, we procrastinate if the rewards for our action aren't immediate and will only materialize in the future, like setting up a 401(k), meditating, or strength training.

While all of these factors in procrastination will arise in our journeys to wellness, the last two: putting off actions that cause discomfort or won't provide immediate gratification, are perhaps the most common forms I witness in clients. Melissa is a prime example.

## Melissa's Story

Many clients come to me when their situation gets too difficult to tolerate, when they've reached some sort of bottom. Years of poor eating and sleeping behaviors, lack of exercise, and other destructive habits have left them sick, achy, tired, and stressed out. But some, like Melissa, approach me to improve a relatively healthy lifestyle. In fact, Melissa was more interested in being a better health role model for her children than reaping any tangible benefits for herself. While this was a wonderful idea in theory, she lacked the motivation that concrete goals may have given her.

Her primary interest was eating healthier. She barely had any fruit or vegetables in her diet and often skipped breakfast or had a biscuit instead. But in session after session she reported that she didn't do the simple task of stopping at the produce stand on her corner on the way to work to pick up fruit to eat with a yogurt for a healthy breakfast at her desk. She also wanted to get fit and stronger. But she put off any steps toward this goal as well. Although she had taken yoga in the past, she was reluctant to make one class a week.

Of course, I wouldn't give up on Melissa. Although she was healthy, I knew that eating better and getting stronger would help her deal with the many stresses in her life—even though she hadn't come to me with that complaint. So we came up with a plan that would stem her procrastination. First, I suggested she place Post-its to remind her to bring a healthy breakfast to work on her alarm clock, bathroom mirror, and handbag. I asked her to report back to me after five days of breakfast how her energy and stress levels were at work, thereby providing a deadline and an interesting experiment. She rose to the challenge. After that trial week, she never missed bringing her breakfast again.

Next, I helped her remember all the wonderful aspects of yoga, helping her envision the things about it that would be pleasurable, relaxing. In other words, more like a treat than a chore. She began going twice a week.

## How to Greet this Obstacle

Procrastinators are usually aware of this characteristic. But all of us could benefit by knowing how often and how intensely we procrastinate. Find a quiet space and try to use mindfulness methods to still your mind. Then consider these questions:

- When you're given a project at work/school do you start right away?
- Do you file your taxes in the final week?
- Do you use a snooze button?
- Is your New Year's Resolution the same every year?
- Has it been more than a year since you went to the dentist?
- Do others need to remind you to complete your part in group projects?
- Does clean laundry sit for more than a day before being put away?
- Are there often dishes in the sink from the day before?
- Does it take more than 24 hours for you to respond to emails?
- Are there items on your to-do list, like writing a will, that have been on there for months or years?

If you answered yes to two or more of these (on a regular basis) then it's time to greet this obstacle.

## How to Apply a Kindful Solution

First, don't beat up on yourself—it won't help and it will actually hurt. In fact, a study published in the journal "Personality and Individual Differences" found that students who forgave themselves for putting off preparing for an exam were less likely to delay preparing for the next exam than those who felt bad about themselves. And negative self-talk will only lead to stress—and we know where that takes us.

Instead, this is the time to apply Kindfulness. Understand that procrastination is based mostly on fear, and it comes naturally. But when it no longer serves us, we can work to try to alleviate it. It will take time, but be patient.

Here's some more good news: Just as procrastinating leads to stress, getting things accomplished, being on time, and being responsible builds a sense of self-esteem and self-trust. And these qualities can lead to greater satisfaction in work, relationships, and your health.

Working with my clients and on my own procrastination issues, I've found these three simple ways to conquer even the most intractable case of procrastination:

### Fake the Clock

If there isn't a deadline, create one. Tell yourself that medical claim needs to be mailed by Monday, and put it in your calendar, reminder app, or to-do list. If you do have a deadline, break it down into smaller units of time: You need to complete the marketing report by Friday, so remind yourself you have only 16 work hours to get it done. If this causes more stress than motivation, move on to the next strategy.

### Bring in a Buddy

If you tell a trusted friend, spouse, or coach that you are committing to painting the bathroom before the end of the weekend, this is often the "secret sauce" to finding your necessary motivation. My clients tell me all the time that they envision themselves proudly announcing their accomplishments to me at our next session and that gets them started whether they're cooking at home, walking to work, or even having a difficult relationship conversation. Further, another person may be able to help you explore and dismantle any fears or hesitation you've been feeling about whatever you've been putting off.

**Break it Down**

This is the strategy I use most often. Instead of seeing the entire enormous project looming over you, remember that you just have to do one small part at a time. If you need to clean the entire house, tell yourself you can start at the living room and give yourself a break after that room is done. I find that people usually continue anyway.

# Obstacle: Unrealistic Expectations

When my clients find out that their first assignment is to drink water upon awakening and take the stairs at work twice a week, they often protest and ask for more to do. Or when they report they only lost one pound they often seem embarrassed by this admirable achievement. They want to run before they can walk (sometimes literally). Why? Because they have enormous or unrealistic expectations of themselves, and therefore find it hard to be satisfied with small victories. We all want big success, but trying to make dramatic changes to your lifestyle quickly will be frustrating, daunting, and will have most folks throwing their hands up in defeat. This is the reason that tried-and-true adages like "every great journey begins with a step" are used so often.

Having high expectations and seeing reasonable results can lead to impatience and frustration. That's why so many people quit diets or new healthy regimens and go back to what's familiar. That is, if they don't have support and accountability.

Then there's the trap of measuring ourselves against unrealistic standards outside of ourselves. In other words, we make unfair comparisons. We all do it and we all suffer, because these comparisons are an easy way to beat up on ourselves, feel defeated, and engage in destructive behaviors.

In case you don't see yourself yet in this description, let me be more specific in describing what I have observed as the three most common comparison traps:

### 1. Measuring Against Others

Whether it's in the yoga studio, workplace, or in relation to friends and family, many of us will measure our skill level or progress against someone else's. We sneak an envious look at someone's seemingly effortless crow pose, wonder why Cindy can do Excel spreadsheets so quickly, berate ourselves for not having Bob's baking acumen, or are stymied why Rachel's dating life is so robust when ours is fizzling.

Not only do these observations cause disappointment and pain, they separate us from our fellow human beings. Feeling inferior (or superior, for that matter) is a way to block intimacy.

### 2. Measuring Against the Past

If you're asking yourself why it takes you a week to bounce back from a long night out, or why you can't do a headstand anymore, then you are suffering from this insidious syndrome. It's just plain fact that our bodies change as we age. Sure, there's a lot we can do to keep ourselves in the best shape possible, but some things are mostly beyond our control, like hormonal changes, decreasing metabolism and immunity, diminishing eyesight and hearing, wrinkles, etc. And sometimes we are just out of practice because our lives have become big and beautiful and we can't devote 10 hours a week to whatever we used to do to stay in shape. Comparing ourselves today to our younger selves is a doozy because besides lowering your self-esteem, it keeps you out of the present moment (mindfulness), out of gratitude and appreciation for what you do have, and in a constant state of frustration because—spoiler—you can't go back in time.

How to stop it: Kill it with Kindfulness. Applying awareness, acceptance, and a new perspective will help you get out of this harmful trap. For example, while the downsides of aging are real and often unwelcome, there's a bright side too: You have gained a lot since you were young—and I'm not talking about weight. Along the line, you've gained wisdom, patience, prudence, self-awareness, confidence, grace, enlightenment, experience, education, you name it.

Seriously…you name it. If you long for your younger self and berate yourself for who you are today, make a list of some positive attributes you've acquired as you've gotten older and I'm sure it will beat being able to run fast any day.

### 3. Measuring Against the Future

If the following scenarios sound familiar, you may be in trouble too: You start a diet and wonder why you haven't lost all the weight in a month; you chide yourself for not having enough money to retire at age 45; you begin weight training and are frustrated that you can't do a dead lift in the first week; you started a job two months ago, and can't believe you haven't gotten a raise yet. Trying to rush the future is a futile task that only brings heartbreak and ultimately defeat. That's why so many people quit their diets, fitness regimens, jobs, and other challenges before reaching their goals.

## How to Greet this Obstacle

We all tend to compare ourselves to others, look back at the past, get a bit too eager about the future, and set high standards and get impatient. But when we do this frequently, without ever appreciating our current state or any kind of progress, then it is an obstacle. Here are some questions to determine if this is your obstacle:

- In exercise classes, do you frequently check out other students?
- Do you look at a high-school classmate's photo on Facebook and wonder why they seem younger looking?
- Have you ever tried to quit smoking cold turkey without help?
- When you invest money, do you check the account more than once a month?
- Have you ever dropped out of a class after the first session because it seemed too difficult to master?
- Do you resent certain coworkers because they are seemingly better at a skill-set or more highly recognized?
- Does it depress you to look at old photos or videos of yourself?
- Have you ever tried a drastic way to lose weight (like at-home cleanses, extreme prolonged fasting, purging, or laxatives)?
- Have you ever bought a celebrity-endorsed product expecting to end up with their body, skin, hair, etc.?
- Do you begin to fantasize about your wedding after dating someone for a week?

If you answered yes to two or more of these then you are probably hurting yourself with unrealistic expectations.

## How to Apply a Kindful Solution

### Get Right-Sized

Take a moment to remind yourself of these absolute facts: Some people are better at some things than you are. They could have more experience, training, easier upbringings, different bodies, or different brains. And guess what, you're better at some things than others. But most important, life isn't a competition.

### Ask for Help

If you are dissatisfied with your yoga practice, office skills, or culinary abilities, ask for extra assistance and only measure your own progress.

## Be Gentle and Patient

It takes a long time for any person to change their behaviors—especially ones that have been ingrained for years or decades. Any progress is a step in the right direction, and more than you've done before. By using patience and understanding—the foundation of Kindfulness—you should be able to stop the negative feelings that can have you on the fast track to throwing in the towel.

## Set Smaller Goals

For example, instead of focusing on the 20 pounds you want to lose, set a goal of eating smaller portions at dinner, or swapping greens for carbs three meals a week, preparing your lunch at home two days a week, and so on. These goals are within your power (unlike losing weight, which can fluctuate depending on your metabolism, hormones, illness, bloating, and other factors). If you do that, the pounds will come off naturally—eventually—but it won't be your focus or the reason for your frustration.

## Acknowledge your Efforts

Give yourself a pat on the back for setting up that 401(k), getting to the gym, and working hard at the office—all the stuff you used to be hard on yourself about. Life can be hard, but unfortunately, we can make it even harder by engaging in unreasonable expectations of ourselves. Appreciate and reward any forward progress to keep yourself motivated.

## Forgive

Give yourself a break when you inevitably regress or mess up. As long as there's a tomorrow, there's opportunity.

In addition to trying these solutions, you can refer to the affirmations in the self-compassion section for more help.

# Obstacle: Fears

Franklin Delano Roosevelt said it best: "We have nothing to fear but fear itself."

We all have fears. It's a natural part of being human, and it can be very helpful in certain situations like when it prevents you from jumping into the lion's cage at the zoo. But often fear is just a bogeyman—a fantasy of what might happen—not reality. And, when this bogeyman stops you from pursuing your dreams, well then, we have a problem.

Fear is perhaps the most common negative emotion because—in my humble opinion and that of many spiritual thinkers—it is behind every other negative emotion. Every one of the so-called seven deadly sins (pride, anger, gluttony, sloth, greed, lust, and envy) has its root in fear. That's because fear can be broken down into two categories that cover most everything: fear of losing what we have, and fear of not getting what we want.

**Fear of Loss**

This isn't as a simple as worrying about leaving your iPhone in an Uber. It can mean fearing death (of yourself or a loved one), illness, injury, divorce, being fired. It can also mean entering a situation that could put your security, identity, integrity, pride, status, or reputation at risk. Fearing pain, discomfort, or awkwardness about anything intimidating or unfamiliar is also a fear of losing what you have. This kind of fear is a common obstacle preventing people from taking steps to get healthier. Frequently, this will crop up as, "I'll never give up_____." Whether it's hamburgers, cake, beer, butter, working late, shopping for sport, I've heard it all. You may be surprised to learn that I've never asked anyone to give up anything as a health coach. But oddly enough, after working on their health for a while, many people start voluntarily abandoning what they used to cherish. For example, night owls start to feel like an early bedtime is a treat when they're good and tired; that new handbag is no longer a temptation for those who want their financial health to match their new-found vigor; all that gas and bloating no longer seems worth it for the former fan of the Friday night beer and burger.

The Kindfulness solution for this expression of fear is to approach the suggestion of giving something up with a different perspective. Realize that no one is going to strip this away from you. But allow yourself to be open to new things and a new life, one in which you may no longer seek to cling to this habit or preference. Don't start with the idea of deprivation, start with the goal of better health and see what happens to your tastes and desires over time. Never say never.

## Paolo's Story

Paolo had long put off seeking help for his weight problem because a nutritionist had once told him that he had to stop eating beans and rice. This was a huge part of his heritage and a serious form of comfort and pleasure for him. I knew that any plan for Paolo that forbade him from eating this food would only lead to frustration and failure. Of course, he did need to alter his diet that included too much fatty meat and large portions of refined carbohydrates (like white rice) if he was to lose the extra pounds he was carrying and get his recently diagnosed Type 2 diabetes under control. So he and I worked together to revise his favorite beans and rice recipe to use smaller amounts of lean meat, brown rice, and lots more beans. We upped the flavor profile by adding spices and herbs authentic to his culture instead of oil, butter, and salt. He realized that he would not lose his ethnic identity or the comfort of the familiar in order to eat better. When the pounds started dropping, and he was feeling more energized and happier, Paolo became more willing to leave behind other less-than-virtuous foods, such as potato chips and bagels, that were holding him back from reaching his goals.

**Fear of Not Getting What We Want (aka Fear of Failure):**

This can be even more insidious, especially for people who don't want to admit any need or feeling of dependency. Going back to the good old seven deadly sins, fear of not getting what we want often makes us desperate or controlling, hoping to edge out others for the object of our desire. This can lead to emotions like envy, resentment, greed, and competition. Worry that we will never be satisfied leads to gluttony, greed, and lust.

As described above, fear of not getting what we want is often expressed as procrastination or perfectionism. We're afraid we won't achieve success, it will be more difficult than we think, or it won't look perfect so we put it off. This fear is paralyzing unless it is addressed with Kindfulness.

When talking to people about their resistance to something like losing weight, I hear fear of failure expressed with this excuse: "Diets don't work for me." This usually means that they have tried a fad diet, failed, and then gained even more weight. Or they tried on their own without support, information, or accountability, and failed. Even though weight loss may be what they want, naming it, desiring it, and then not getting it—yet again—is just too frightening and prevents them from trying again.

Oddly there is another fear that one wouldn't think exists, but does. And that's fear of success. It's a potent combination of fear of loss and fear of not getting one's needs met. Those who fear success are usually people who—on some level—don't believe that they deserve attention, rewards, and achievement. They are often more familiar with loss, depression, and deprivation and feel safer in that state. They fear the judgment of others and new responsibilities or situations that their success may bring. I first saw this when coaching Alice.

## Alice's Story

Alice is a wonderfully kind and spiritual person in her late 40s. She had lost both of her parents and her husband early in life. She had also switched careers and moved a few times. When she came to me, she had just shuttered a business and wanted to get in better shape before looking for a new job that wouldn't be as sedentary. She also said she was ready for a new relationship and wanted to feel more attractive. She was intelligent, receptive, and incredibly willing. She took suggestions eagerly, stuck to her exercise and food goals, and lost weight easily and consistently for several weeks. But then she stopped. It was as if I were coaching a completely different person. She started eating ice cream every night, no longer took her daily walk, and used any excuse to indulge in large "celebratory meals." We began to talk more about what was going on in her life and she began complaining about all the extra attention she was getting now that she had lost 15 pounds—especially from men. While none of it was inappropriate, she said she was uncomfortable being judged that way. Together we realized that Alice had been using her extra weight as a way to hide from the public and stay in a state of living that she had grown accustomed to—even though part of her wanted out.

Gently, I helped Alice see her contradictory needs and grow more comfortable with the idea of living a new life. Instead of focusing on her changing looks we decided to place an emphasis on greater health to spur her on. She posted notes on her fridge that read, "Each pound I lose means 10 less pounds of pressure on my joints" and other forms of motivation. We also used affirmations, meditation, and prayer to remind her that she was in control of who she would date and any other aspect of her life. I also encouraged her to surround herself with loving, supportive people who would help her feel secure during her transformation.

What was also at work in Alice's story was the fear that success would turn her into something she didn't want to be. In addition to getting unwanted attention, maybe others wouldn't like her or would envy her for becoming more "attractive." People like Alice fear abandoning the life they have now—even if it is unsatisfying. In so many ways, this fear is perhaps the most menacing of the "bogeymen."

## How to Greet this Obstacle

Because we all experience fear, we must engage in mindfulness to see if fear of losing something precious, fear that we will not get what we want or in the way we want it, or fear that transformation will lead us to become something we don't deserve or can't accept is blocking us from taking steps toward greater health and satisfaction. Noticing when fears crop up in a daily journal or meditation practice is enormously helpful. I also suggest creating a list of what you'd like to achieve in life, what things you fear losing, what makes you feel safe, and what makes you feel like you. Knowing these things will allow you to identify if you think they are threatened and if that fear is real or not.

If you need some help getting started you can also consider the questions below. But because the subject of fear is so varied, use these only as a jumping off point, not a precise measurement.

- Do you tend to see the negatives first when someone makes a suggestion?
- Have you wanted to make a big move (end a relationship, move homes, quit a job) but can't envision a better life?
- Are you afraid that getting healthier will mean sacrificing your favorite foods?
- Do you believe that exercise will hurt or feel like drudgery?
- Do you think losing weight/sleeping better is harder for someone like you?
- Do you believe that your family and friends won't like you or want

to spend time with you if you cease to engage in behaviors that they do (overeating, drinking, overspending)?

- Do you feel that others will mock your attempts to get healthier as vain or frivolous?

- Do think you'll have to give up all sources of fun or pleasure to be healthier?

- Are you worried you'll have success in quitting an unhealthy habit only to relapse?

- Do you believe getting healthier will cost you too much time or money?

## How to Apply a Kindful Solution

When confronting a fear of losing what we have, it's important to incorporate Kindfulness. First, we recognize and are respectful of this fear. Next, we take the following actions:

### Affirmations

You can repeat to yourself, "I don't need to hold on to this. I no longer need it."

### Reality Check

Remind yourself that you are safe and that all your needs are taken care of. You can also write down the worst-case scenario of loss, including what you would need from yourself and others to help you get through it.

### Show Gratitude

Identify a small reward for yourself once you've accomplished an activity you've feared.

### Build a Team

Ask for help, support, or advice if you need it. It's not cheating if someone holds your hand during a scary new venture.

For fear of loss, try to give yourself the respect, patience, and understanding you deserve so you can learn to apply Kindfulness. Remember that if you have "failed" or suffered the disappointment of not reaching your goals in the past with quick solutions like fad diets or packaged plans, you are not alone. They don't work for most people over the long term. So step one is to forgive yourself and remember your humanity.

Keep in mind that what will work going forward is learning about healthy foods and reasonable portions, exploring reasons for destructive behaviors and habits, sleeping better, reducing stress, finding ways to incorporate movement into your life, and living in a way that exemplifies self-compassion. Keep in mind that you—as a human—will always experience temporary setbacks and regressions but that is not a loss, it's an obstacle. If you learn real self-care, you will have a sustainable plan for living that can never be taken away. Which means there is no failure, and therefore, nothing to fear.

Fear of success can also lead people to suffer from imposter syndrome, to wonder if they belong, deserve, or will be able to exist in their new healthier life. That is why practicing Kindfulness is absolutely essential in tackling this form of fear. Getting in touch with this by cultivating our own worth and giving ourselves the patience and understanding to overcome this fear can be incredibly effective.

When confronting fear of success, practicing Kindfulness with affirmations that start with "I deserve" and "I can" will give you the strength and assurance that change will be not only acceptable but exciting and deeply satisfying.

# Final Words on Obstacles

As I mentioned at the opening of this chapter, these are the more common obstacles I've encountered in my own life and in coaching clients. Hopefully you identified with some descriptions and stories and are applying Kindfulness as a way to move on.

Or perhaps you have used mindfulness and self-compassion techniques to discover other obstacles and fears. I encourage you to continue with this important work, even as we move forward.

In the next chapter, I will offer you some tried-and-true techniques for accomplishing your health and life goals no matter what they are.

# 6

# REACHING YOUR GOALS KINDFULLY

*"It's impossible for women to have it all,*
*if they have to do it all."*

—Gloria Steinem

I promised you on the cover of this book that the Kindfulness Solution would allow you to transform your body and your life. I'm ready to make good on that promise.

In previous chapters, I've offered strategies and plans to help you cultivate greater mindfulness and self-compassion, and I've laid out the most common obstacles to reaching your goals. Hopefully you've identified—or are beginning to identify—with one, two, or many of them, and are ready to move on to prepare yourself for change.

Whether that change is losing weight, eating healthier, building a stronger body, managing stress, leaving a unsatisfying job or relationship, learning to sleep better, going back to school, or dropping destructive behaviors like smoking, overspending, and more, you can apply the Kindfulness Solution to help us achieve your goals.

All you need now is to take some simple steps to clear a path to success.

# Step 1: Stake Your Claim

Most of us—especially parents and other natural caretakers—will need to make an essential mental shift before we can gather the tools and ingredients for change. Not all the planets need to align for you to begin to eat healthier, get stronger, drop bad habits, lose weight, manage stress, or sleep better. But you will find all this easier if you have made a commitment to focus on yourself and your long-term goals.

Think of it like adopting a dog. All the books tell you that you need to prepare your home and your life for this wonderful—but responsibility-filled—addition. You need to ensure that you have extra money for food and vet bills in your budget. You should make sure that the rest of the family is on board. And you should have a bed or space for the dog to feel safe and secure. But what's actually most important is you. Do you have the time, energy, and desire to give your new pup the exercise, discipline, love, and attention it requires and deserves?

The same is true for learning to finally practice proper self-care and undergo a body and life transformation. While it's helpful to have the extra cash for exercise equipment, organic food, or personal coaching, it's more essential that you are ready to devote more time, energy, and love to yourself—to make yourself, your life, and your body a priority. I like to call this "staking your claim."

For many of us, turning inward or choosing to focus on ourselves can seem selfish—or even out and out irresponsible. But it's quite the opposite. If we devote too much time and energy caring for others and ignore ourselves, we are likely to face a host of problems including weight gain, fatigue, stress, and insomnia—and that's just the beginning. We will certainly be in no shape—mentally, emotionally, or physically—to carry out our jobs or tend to our families and loved ones. And even if we are able to carry on without help or giving ourselves a break, we are at risk for becoming resentful and bitter toward those in our care. That's why you put your oxygen mask on first.

As they always instruct on flights, you must put your oxygen mask on yourself before you can assist another. In other words, if you want to be helpful, to be responsible, and to be there in a crisis, you must have taken care of your own needs first.

It isn't about abandoning others, it's about making yourself a priority. It is a shift in perspective. To help bring about this shift, we must apply Kindfulness. Among the best Kindfulness tools for this job are affirmations. Starting the day by saying a loving and encouraging affirmation to yourself such as, "I love myself enough to be responsible for my own health and wellbeing," is a powerful way to stake your claim.

You may choose another Kindfulness solution. Perhaps you'll ask for a spiritual shift in your prayers or meditation. Or you might refer to the "Get to Know Yourself" section, so you can learn to know—and love—yourself better as a way to want to make yourself a priority. Or you might feel that employing forgiveness techniques is needed first to clear the past and be ready to move forward.

Those of you who are more action-oriented may decide that doing the assignments in the "Cultivating Self-Compassion" chapter and the exercises in the "Greeting Your Obstacles" chapter are ways to demonstrate your commitment to yourself and your shift in thinking.

As I always say in my practice, "Whatever works for you is the right choice!"

Once you've made yourself a priority you are ready to move on to the next steps.

# Step 2: Assemble Your Team

It may take a "village" to raise a child, but it takes a team to keep me healthy. It's ironic, but I have discovered that the secret to successful self-care is help from others. Race-car drivers have pit crews, pitchers have catchers who know just when to ask for the curve ball, candidates have tireless pollsters and canvassers, and Oscar acceptance speeches have taught us that actors have managers, agents, publicists, stylists, and more to thank.

For me, self-care often involves asking for help or seeking out the expertise, counsel, skills—and especially support and accountability—of other beings (sometimes human, sometimes canine!). That's why, over the years, I've assembled my "team." It includes my husband, my dog, my primary care physician, acupuncturist, yoga and meditation teachers, a few select friends, and my peer coach, Frances. What's a peer coach, you may ask?

During my studies at the Institute for Integrative Nutrition, I and my fellow students were encouraged to find our own health coaches to help us not only with our health goals but as a support as we grew our practices. I'm so lucky to have found Frances, a health coach who graduated from the Institute with me. In addition to being close in age and growing up in Brooklyn, Frances and I share a similar sensibility, work ethic, dedication to our health and our clients, love of food, enthusiasm for trying new things, and—most important—sense of humor.

As health coaches (or peer coaches) for each other we help each other reach and maintain our health and health coaching goals. While she provides an invaluable source of inspiration, ideas, and encouragement, Frances also holds me accountable for the goals I set for myself. This means if I feel tempted to walk into Dunkin' Donuts (and who doesn't?) or I'm putting off preparing for a workshop I'm hosting, I know that I will eventually need to report this to her. Knowing this helps keep me on the straight and narrow.

By the same principle, every time I reach a goal or achieve some sort of success, I know she will celebrate with me. As the old saying goes, "A problem shared is halved, and a victory shared is doubled."

In addition to accountability and mentorship, I believe we also need team members who can rally us when we feel we have nothing to give, people who bring us joy and push us to go the extra mile when we have other plans. That's where my husband, friends, and dog come in. My husband will often remind me when I've gone off the deep end and I'm working too much. My dog will force me to go out on long walks and provide a source of laughter and joy. And my friends have encouraged me, listened to me, and been a sounding board for fears and dreams every step of the way. They are my greatest cheerleaders who continue to believe in what I'm doing when I'm beginning to lose faith.

Now it's your turn to build a team. And for you caretaker type-As like me who think they can skip this step, think again. If you're going to attempt real, lasting change, you're going to need a team. Going it alone is more than tough, it is self-defeating.

I know. I've done the "superwoman" gig. I tackled the stressful job while feeding my husband, caring for my ailing parents, cleaning the house, being the shoulder for friends in crisis, doing volunteer work, and trying to keep up with the news. The only thing I ignored was myself and it caught up to me with weight gain, insomnia, and digestive issues.

So take some time—right now works—to assemble your team in your head. Scroll through your contacts and friends on social media, look at an old address book, remember those who've helped you in the past. Perhaps you want to call upon former therapists, doctors, healers, teachers, coaches, clergy, or other helpers for support. Think about gathering some role models as well. If you want to get fit, why not spend more time with your friends who run and bike? If you want to eat better, ask the friendly coworker who always brings in a fabulous-looking grain salad for lunch to sit with you and share her recipe.

Just make sure that these are folks who lift your spirits, encourage you to be your best, make you laugh, and acknowledge just how great you are. Try to see these folks in person, instead of using social media, texting, and emailing as your main sources of communication. I recently read that the Dalai Lama said, "I think technology makes a lot of things much easier. But technology cannot produce compassion." In other words, a tweet will never replace a hug.

Of course, you can always try to wrangle a friend or family member to join you in your transformation. For some people, it can be more fun to have a buddy to compare notes, share ideas, celebrate achievements, and commiserate with. The only caveat is to be sure you focus on your progress, not theirs. And if they decide to throw in the towel, you keep going.

If you get stuck trying to figure out your team, just fantasize about your Oscar or Nobel Prize acceptance speech. Who would you thank for getting you where you are today? Not out of a sense of obligation, but because they were there when the going got rough, they inspired you, they had your back. Those folks should be your first draft picks for your team.

# Step 3: Carve Out Time

As I've mentioned before, time is a common excuse for staying stuck. I often find that people have the time, but they use "lack of time" to cover for a fear, uncertainty, or other mental block. Even for those busy folks who are indeed time-strapped, there are usually solutions. Sure, cooking at home, working out, studying, reading, seeing therapists, going to classes, and meditating are all time-consuming, but this shouldn't deter you.

The time needed to accomplish these tasks is usually much less than people fear. Even more important, people can usually carve out time if they are able to cut down on their "time-sucks"—activities that seem pleasurable or necessary but are mostly wasteful and inefficient. Here are just a few suggestions to eliminate or decrease common time-sucks:

### 1. Limit TV, Social Media, and Phone Games

When I was preparing this book, I took an informal survey of my friends, clients, and newsletter readers about what they considered the worst time-sucks. The number-one answer—by far!—was Facebook. As we drift from one interesting post to another, reading articles and watching silly cat videos, we are blissfully unaware of the minutes flying by. The same is true for phone games and binge-watching Netflix. Limiting your time on screens by setting an alarm or just prohibiting them on some days can give you back many hours in the week.

### 2. Telecommute

If you spend an hour or more going back and forth to work each day, see if you can telecommute one or two days a week or work flex hours (e.g., four ten-hour days instead of five eight-hour days) to have a full day off.

### 3. Get Professional Help

Refer back to the "lighten your load" section of the "Cultivating Self-Compassion" chapter to see if you can hire someone to clean your house, do your laundry, mow your lawn, or take on periodic tasks like filing your taxes, fixing a slow computer, or painting. They'll do it quicker, better, and save you massive headaches—and probably money—today and in the future.

### 4. Drop Perfectionism

Researching the best nail salon, the most convenient flight, or the best deal on a mattress can take hours. Going with "good enough" saves time and energy.

### 5. Delegate or Automate

Roaming the supermarket, pet store, or drug store aisles takes a lot of time, but setting up a repeating order on online sites like Fresh Direct, Vitacost, Chewy, and more is super fast. Or ask your spouse, roommate, or kids to take this task on once in a while. This can apply to other chores like paying bills.

### 6. Plan Ahead

Your meals, outfits, workouts, and social engagements can all be planned in advance and set to repeat, cutting the time involved in decision-making and planning. For example, in my home, meals are scheduled like this: Monday is vegetarian, Tuesday is fish, Wednesday is dinner salad, and so on.

### 7. Limit Work Outside of the Office

Unless it's a crisis, leave your work behind at night: no calls, texts, emails, or reading for the job. If you feel guilty, keep in mind that whatever you are doing to make yourself happier and healthier will make you a sharper—and more easy-going—worker.

To figure out which of the above strategies you can apply to your own life to find time for a healthier you, I suggest keeping a log of all your daily activities for one full week. Yes, everything—from showering, getting dressed, preparing meals, reading the paper, checking

Facebook, commuting, and so on throughout the day. Then you can better analyze which activities are taking an inordinate amount of time. It's a little tedious, but it's also a valuable process of discovery. If you find that you stopped at the grocery store on your way home from work three days a week, could you cut that down to one trip if you planned ahead and made a list? Does it convince you to consider a supermarket delivery service? Did you go out of your way to fill up your gas tank because you ignored the gauge until the warning light came on? Choose a gas station that is on one of your regular routes and fill up once a week whether you're on E or not.

Once you see where you can cut time-sucks, you can carve out time for the activities that will help you move forward on the path to transformation. Full steam ahead!

# Step 4: Clear the Decks

In order to prepare a beautiful meal from scratch, you must first clear the counter. Every chef and amateur cook knows that it's much easier to prep this way and avoid spills, cuts, burns, contamination, and mess. In addition, it sharpens your focus.

Now it's time to do the same with your home and life. It's time to clear away things that can cause you harm, distract you, and disrupt your attempts at getting healthier. As with kitchen clutter, some things can go right in the trash while others can be put in their proper place or out of sight.

I like to start with certain people. Have you ever noticed that spending time with some people can leave you feeling sapped and depressed? I call them "emotional vampires" because they suck the life out of you. They dump their problems on your lap, focus on the superficial, engage in gossip or denigrate others, contradict everything you say, and often poop on your hopes and dreams.

Although you may love them or feel some sort of obligation to these folks, as you focus on yourself and your health, it will be immensely helpful to limit interaction with these detractors as best you can. I know it may not be easy. If your boss, spouse, or best friend is a source of constant criticism or is bringing you down…well, it might be time for a serious talk, a parting of the ways, or a break.

Even friends and family who seem positive, loving, and supportive may seek to distract you from your goals. It may be difficult to comprehend, but there are people who claim to love you but will be threatened by your attempts to move on and improve yourself. It's sad, but true. They may not even be aware of it on a conscious level. You need to protect yourself from their attempts to subtly—and blatantly—sabotage your efforts. This may sound familiar: "Oh, come on. You've been so good. You can have one (cookie, beer, cigarette, fill in the blank)." In these cases, I like to remember that "no" is a one-word answer. Just keep smiling, remembering your goals, your commitment to yourself, and say "no," (or "no, thanks," if that feels easier). But if they persist, these folks will need to take a back seat for a while.

Now, onto the tangible items that can disrupt and distract you. Let's start with food. If you're trying to lose weight or just get healthier, go through the fridge and pantry and toss out any junk. Gather main offenders like potato chips, candy, cookies, cakes, and ice cream, but also examine the labels on stuff like salad dressings, sauces, yogurts, cereal, and so-called energy or snack bars for excessive amounts of added sugar (more than 8 or 9 grams per serving is excessive). If you share your home with others who are not on board, then try to ensure that these foods are at least tucked away out of sight. Toss moldy or wilted veggies and fruit, questionable jars of capers living in the back of the fridge, ancient spices and oils, and any expired foods on your shelves or with freezer-burn. This will make your food supply more attractive and efficient and give you a better chance at eating healthy.

Clearing the decks of junk around your house is the next secret weapon in your fight to get healthier. I know it sounds weird, but multiple studies have shown an astonishing connection between clutter and stress and destructive behaviors. Are your shelves, tables, floors, or dressers spilling over with books, magazines, mail, paperwork, receipts, recent purchases, old electronics, dusty knick-knacks, empty boxes, etc.? You may not realize that this clutter can cause underlying anxiety that leads to overeating and more.

It can also be such a distraction that it stops you from starting anything new and healthy, so one of your final steps is to clear the clutter. It's hard to get good habits like exercise and cooking going when you can't find your sneakers or your kitchen's a mess. File those bills and paperwork, donate read books, recycle the magazines, and find permanent spots for everything else. Pay special attention to your bedroom, and try to remove clutter and unnecessary electronics (see the next chapter for more details).

You might not need to do all of this, or to do all of this at once. Making progress on the areas that affect you most strongly is what's important. And when you can, ask for assistance.

Clearing the decks should provide a sense of calm that will positively affect your eating habits and stress levels and get you ready for the work ahead.

## Step 5: Set Smart Goals

Now that you're ready to dig in to the work of transformation, how do you go about it? Here's where most folks get stymied. Lack of vision or a too-big vision can lead to paralysis. You need a plan, but don't try to do so much at once that you get overwhelmed and quit. (If this sounds like you, it might be worth reviewing the section on unrealistic expectations in the "Greet Your Obstacles" chapter.)

In health coaching sessions, my clients and I break down their larger goals into smaller steps—steps that my health coaching school, the Institute of Integrative Nutrition, refers to as SMART goals. This stands for Specific, Measurable, Attainable, Realistic, and Timely.

I'll give you an example. Rebecca wanted to start exercising after years of being sedentary, and mentioned she had a pool in her high-rise building. She wanted her goal for the next two weeks to be to swim 20 minutes, twice a week, in that pool. I agreed, although it actually seemed ambitious. She reported two weeks later that she hadn't swum at all. When I asked why, she sighed and gave me a list of excuses, which included that she didn't know the schedule of the pool and didn't have a swimsuit that fit. So her goals for the following two weeks became purchasing a swimsuit and procuring the pool schedule.

Of course, there were also underlying fears and other obstacles involved in her inability to fulfill her first goal. But when she was given SMART goals, she could easily complete her tasks without hesitation because they were realistic, tangible, and less intimidating. This allowed her to feel a sense of achievement and to experience forward momentum while we addressed those obstacles.

I have found in my practice that SMART goals provide focus, enhance productivity, bolster self-esteem, and increase commitment. So when you are about to begin your own health transformation journey, clearly outline the series of steps for achieving it to stay on track and reduce feeling overwhelmed. These goals can easily be adjusted as you go.

Here are questions you can ask to ensure your goals are SMART:

### Is this goal Specific?

Be as detailed as possible. The more information you supply, the better your chance at success. Include the following: Who is involved? What do you want to accomplish? When? Where? Why? For example, "I want to exercise more" is not specific and feels unmanageable and intimidating. However, "I want to walk on the treadmill for 20 minutes at the Equinox gym on Main Street on Monday, Wednesday, and Friday, right after work, starting December 1st" is specific and defined. Are there any requirements and/or constraints that will prevent you from taking actionable steps toward reaching the target goal? For example, will you need to join Equinox? Do you have a meeting after work on Wednesday? You might need to back up and make a new goal of joining the gym first, followed by rescheduling the meeting or workout date.

### Is this goal Measurable?

"Eating better" is hard to measure. Cutting out dessert four nights a week is measurable.

### Is this goal Attainable?

In other words, do you have the access, time, energy, skill, money, or whatever is needed to achieve the goal? If not, reassess or try to find those resources.

### Is this goal Realistic?

Check in with yourself using Kindfulness tools to make sure you're not overreaching. Spending two weeks on an easier or simpler goal won't hurt. Remember, this is a lifetime journey, not a sprint.

### Is this goal Timely?

Anchor your goal with a deadline, and mark each deadline in your planner to stay on track. Health coaching sessions are every other week. The client's deadline is usually the next meeting. You may choose to give yourself shorter or longer deadlines depending on the task. But try not to push yourself too hard or procrastinate.

One last word about goals...and it's important, so listen up:

In addition to being SMART, your goals—both large and small—must also be things you WANT to do. If you hate walking on a treadmill, for example, find an alternative. (See the next chapter for exercise ideas.) Survey friends for ideas. Remember to try new things until you find what fits for you. Sample and sample and sample again. And don't let prejudice stop you. (You can go back for a "prejudice" refresher in the "Greet Your Obstacles" chapter.)

Remember, there's no rush. Small, incremental, attainable changes are easier, gentler, and—most important—sustainable over the long run. So if you're ready to change your body and live a healthier life, start with small steps.

# Step 6: Use Gadgets, Tricks, and Tools

As you set out on the road toward positive transformation, it's good to have some tricks up your sleeve for when the going gets tough. And if you've lived on planet Earth for a while, you may have noticed that the going does indeed get tough from time to time.

I've learned to employ an arsenal of gadgets, tricks, and tools to help me stay on track with my health and help me go from goal to goal more easily. It's like adding a super hero—or two—to your team.

Let's start with gadgets!

If you're hoping to increase your movement, lose weight, manage stress, and sleep better, you are living in the right era. It seems every day a new gadget is invented for folks who want to improve their health and lives, and drop destructive habits.

Here's a short list, some of which my clients and I have used personally, and others that come highly recommended:

## MyFitness Pal

This is the most popular food-logging/calorie-counting app, and it can link to fitness trackers and other programs to seamlessly give you a tally of calories consumed and other stats like macronutrients (fat, protein, and carbs), micronutrients (vitamins and minerals), hydration, and calories burned. Even if your goal is to simply eat healthier this app is truly your pal. I used it on my weight-loss journey and will pick it up when I have a backslide. There can be a learning curve, but once you get accustomed to it and have entered your favorite foods and recipes once, it is easy and invaluable. If you just can't get over the hump, move on.

## Fitness Trackers

You've probably noticed more and more people are wearing bands and watch-like devices on their wrists to count their steps. These handy devices can also track sleep patterns, walk you through meditations and workouts, prompt you to walk, remind you of appointments, and give you medical data like heart rate. If you are motivated by numbers and competitive with yourself (wanting to top your previous step count, etc.) this should help you.

## Meditation Apps

Two very popular apps, "Headspace" and "Mindfulness," offer free versions that provide guided and timed meditations. They'll also send you inspiring messages and prompts to meditate. If stress management, lowering blood pressure, or greater mindfulness are among your goals, these can help you with motivation and ideas.

## Finance Apps

Mint is the most popular app for budget-tracking. There are other investment apps as well. If your goal involves decreasing spending or getting smarter about your financial life, try one of these. They provide accountability, organization, and tips.

## Exercise Apps

There are apps for every kind of workout. I've used "7 Minutes," which takes you through movements like squats and jumping jacks in seven-minute cycles. I like this one because it allows me to squeeze in a workout practically anywhere, at any time.

## Accountability Apps

I've read about apps like "stickK" that help you with accountability by serving you with a monetary punishment if you don't do what you pledged you would. The money goes to a charity, a person you designate (like a bet!), or an "anti-charity" (one whose views you disagee with). I can't totally recommend this, because I'd prefer that everyone get to the bottom of why they can't meet their goals (see the chapters on Obstacles and Self-Compassion). And to me, punishment is not Kindfulness. But if you are having trouble getting started, you could try this while you are digging deep into your blocks.

## Period Trackers

For women who want a better handle on their hormones and whose menstrual cycles affect their emotions, digestion, and other body functions, there are some great apps out there. Some focus on fertility and others on health or mood.

This list is based on topics that have interested my clients and me. If you have other goals—digestion, smoking, nail biting, or something else—there's an ever-growing number of apps that can help you break bad habits and reinforce good ones. An online search will turn up lists of the best and newest.

Now on to tools…

A worker is only as good as her tools. So whatever your goal is, make sure you have all the tools you need on hand. For example, if you want to do yoga, having your own mat and proper clothes will help you feel prepared and reinforce your overall investment in this goal. I believe that everyone should have some light hand-weights at home for when they can't get to the gym. And my husband and many others swear by bands for resistance training—which you can take with you when you travel.

Sleeping better may require investing in tools to create a better sleep environment. (We'll explore this fully in Chapter 7.)

Those who want to cook more and eat healthier will need tools like cutting boards, knives, pots and pans, measuring cups, and a kitchen scale. The last two are invaluable if you have an issue with portion control or aren't that familiar with portions. And with food like rice, accidentally doubling the portion can mean an extra 150 calories. That adds up over time. Learn to measure until you can accurately eyeball it. Like starting school with a fresh new notebook and pens, having the right tools on hand means you will start off on the right foot and won't get delayed with trips to the store (or convenient excuses!). Here are a couple of tools my clients have used to keep themselves on track:

**Journals or Vision Boards**

Vision boards are personal creations, or collages, using images (magazine pages, photos, drawings) and words to illustrate your goals. If your goal is to get a stronger, fitter body, your vision board may have images of lean folks climbing mountains, running, and more with inspiring messages like "dream big" or "every journey begins with a single step." It may sound cheesy but putting this board in plain view is a great reminder. You can take it down when others visit. And, recording your thoughts and feelings in a journal, whether it's daily, weekly, or periodically is another creative way to get clearer on your goals and obstacles and measure your progress.

**Social Media**

This can also be a great tool if used properly. If it is a time-suck (see above) or a trigger for feelings of envy or resentment, then you need to leave it behind or learn how to use it for a better purpose. As a tool in self-improvement, social media can help with accountability, support, information, and inspiration. By posting your goals—smaller steps or your larger goal—on Facebook, let's say, you are letting the world know and you will feel obliged to keep them abreast of your progress. In fact, you can tell them you will report back to them weekly. Remember, you may be inspiring them, too.

When you hit blocks or feel discouraged, you can also post your issue and look for support. Believe me, whatever you're going through, someone else has been there and knows how to get out. Or at least can offer empathy.

If you're looking for inspiration for healthy meals, yoga poses, meditation methods, smoking cessation techniques, and more, learn to use social media hashtags on Instagram, Twitter, and other sites to find ideas, pertinent articles, recipes, and more. The world is your encyclopedia. And it's all free! Go for it!

OK, you've got the tools, now here are some tricks I've developed along the way:

## The "Seefood" Diet

The foods we see are the foods we eat. To eat healthy, keep a bowl of fresh fruit on your kitchen counter or dining table. I also keep a Mason jar or two of nuts nearby to keep me from digging into potato chips when I feel like something salty or crunchy or a quick snack. The same is true for your exercise equipment, books, or anything that's part of your healthy life plan. Keep them in sight and handy.

## Rewards

All work and no play is no way to treat yourself Kindfully. Further, it will likely lead to burnout. Rewarding yourself for reaching an important goal is not only a great way to show some love to yourself, but it will keep you on track. My experience has shown that incentivizing things like diet, exercise, or quitting a bad habit strengthens commitment. The problem is that many of us have learned to reward ourselves in less-than virtuous ways. For example, when we have a rough day at work, we cuddle up with Ben & Jerry. When we finally finish that onerous project, we celebrate with a bottle of Moët or a pricey purchase. While this may feel good in the moment, we are then left with hangovers, tummy issues, and regrets—at best. And we are no closer to achieving goals like weight loss and a stronger body. That's why I help clients find new ways to reward and comfort themselves that fit with their likes and dislikes. Here are just a few ideas:

- Take the day off
- Have a Netflix movie marathon
- Go to a concert or play
- Visit an aquarium or museum
- Go to the beach or lake
- Plan a boys/girls night out
- Get a massage
- Get yourself groomed (man-scaping, a mani-pedi, or waxing, hair cut or color)
- Take a steam or swim
- Buy yourself flowers

**Schedule it!**

We are careful to schedule work meetings and doctors' appointments and fit the rest of our lives around them. When you make change a priority, all activities involved should take their place in your calendar as well. If you are committed to exercising three days a week, book it at the beginning of each week (e.g., yoga Tuesday night at 7 p.m.; spin class Thursday at lunch; power toning Saturday at 3 p.m.). Use the alerts and notifications on your phone to remind you of these commitments. You can schedule meditation and journaling time, calls you want to make to your team, research you want to do, courses you want to take, and so on. Booking it makes that time sacrosanct, a solemn promise you make to yourself and keep because you care enough about your wellbeing. That is why it is another illustration of Kindfulness.

**Post-Its**

Digital reminders are great and I use them all the time, but there's something wonderfully persistent about good old-fashioned Post-it notes. They are friendly little pastel-colored drill sergeants you can use to remind you to bring your prepared salad to work for lunch, give you a boost of self-esteem and inspiration on your bathroom mirror each morning, keep you away from less-than virtuous foods in your fridge and pantry, help you stay focused on your goals, and remind you of your upcoming reward (three more days until beach day!). As another bonus, it's not your voice nagging you, it's the Post-it. This way, you can continue to move away from self-berating and move closer to Kindfulness.

Finally, I have a special category of tricks just for warding off cravings. Whether you are trying to eat healthier, give up cigarettes or alcohol, or even exit a toxic relationship, you will at times be drawn to that thing you want to abandon. What you need is to delay the craving and keep busy. Here are some tricks I've offered to clients for when their cravings inevitably begin shouting in their ears:

- Drink a huge glass of water
- Take a walk
- Brush your teeth
- Occupy your hands by giving yourself a manicure, knitting, doing a jigsaw puzzle, or other activity
- Call a friend
- Clean your house
- Have a cup of tea
- Put on music and sing or dance (or both)
- Meditate or breathe
- Take a nap
- Play with your kids or pet

**One last thought before you turn to the next chapter:**

You've staked your claim, assembled your team, cleared the decks, carved out time, learned to set SMART goals, and gotten the insider's scoop on some valuable, time-tested gadgets, tools, and tricks to stay on track. Do you feel ready?

I hope you said yes! Then you can move on to the next chapter, which will outline my Five Pillars of Healthy Living. This mini-guide to a healthy lifestyle can help anyone, regardless of their specific goal, to transform their body and practice Kindfulness.

If you didn't say yes, that's OK! This is a lot to digest. Perhaps it is time for you to take a step back and repeat (or try) some exercises in cultivating self-compassion or greeting your obstacles. It's perfectly normal to identify your personal solution after reading or practicing something multiple times instead of just once.

Remember, this book is your friend. Call upon it as many times as you wish. It will be with you always when you need it. Reading the different chapters and sections again and again, you will find that the friendship changes and grows like any good, sustaining relationship.

# 7

# KEEPING KINDFULLY HEALTHY

*"You, yourself, as much as anybody in the Universe,
deserve your love and attention."*

—Buddha

## Real Self-Care for Busy Bodies

Now that you are beginning to incorporate Kindfulness as a means to reach your goals, you can apply this vital principle to living a healthy life going forward.

You can use mindfulness to stay aware of what your body is saying and whether you are out of balance, tired, ill, or injured. And you can apply self-compassion to carve out the time and devote the gentle energy required to give yourself what you need and deserve to stay healthy and live Kindfully. Some days this might mean pushing yourself to try new things or increase your movement. Other times, it might mean slowing down, resting, and taking mental breaks. Only you will know how to care for you.

Living Kindfully also means placing a focus on real self-care today and every day. When I started my health coaching practice, Well Beings with Karen Azeez, I chose the tagline "Real Self-Care for Busy Bodies" because I wanted to emphasize that no matter how many responsibilities we have in the world and how active our lives are, we should all understand, embrace, and practice basic, real self-care.

When I say "real self-care," I am trying to distinguish it from self-indulgence (see Chapter 3, "The Self-Compassion Quandary"), fad diets, and quick fixes, and doing the bare minimum to stay alive. Real self-care is taking responsibility for your health, growth, and vitality the way you would care for a child, and building strong and consistent habits. This can be challenging for those of us who have long ignored our own needs or have chosen to treat our bodies like factories or amusement parks rather than temples. It's even difficult for those who feel they have done an adequate job of caring for themselves but don't feel that they are living at their optimum.

For all of you...no fears, I've got you covered with some simple suggestions to keep you fit, calm, energized, and living Kindfully.

## The Five Pillars of Self-Care

In a hilarious scene in one of my favorite movies, "Raising Arizona," an ex-con who's desperate to be a father steals a baby from a rich family who has just had quintuplets. Alarms blaring, he scoops up the baby and rushes out, but risks getting caught in order to stop and grab the copy of *Dr. Spock's Baby and Child Care* on the nightstand. Throughout the movie, this baby trades hands again and again and no matter how little time they have or how many people are in pursuit, each kidnapper snatches the book to be sure they take the "instructions."

I get it. Raising a human isn't easy—and it doesn't get easier as we grow up, either. We all wish we had an instruction manual—especially when the going gets tough. If I'm tired for seemingly no reason, I could just turn to page 329 for "Karen's Tired: Cause and Treatment. "

But we don't come with instruction manuals. Even sites like WebMD fall short—because one size definitely does not fit all. What to do?

Over the years, I've realized that no matter our gender, age, activity level, or ethnic background we all need to focus on five aspects of self-care in order to maintain the foundation of a healthy life. Once I identified these important areas—which I refer to as the Five Pillars of Self-Care—I began to lecture and write about them extensively to try to bring this makeshift instruction manual to as many people as possible.

I call these principles the Five Pillars because I envision them working together to hold us up. And as with a structure held up by five pillars, if one of your pillars is shaky, the others can hold the weight, but if two or more are missing or weak, you might slowly collapse or crumble (or at least feel that way). If all five are strong, then you are like a fortress and can take on whatever comes your way.

Working to incorporate all Five Pillars into your life at first may feel like a juggling act. I promise that after a while it will just feel like living, the way that dressing yourself, brushing your teeth, taking a shower, and opening your mail on a daily basis doesn't feel oppressive or awkward. It just is. What will feel different is you!

If you can have all Five Pillars of Self-Care in your life, you will feel more energized, focused, optimistic, calm, and strong. They are as much of an instruction manual as I can give to live your life Kindfully and with robust health.

The Five Pillars of Self-Care can also be helpful (no guarantee, unfortunately) for warding off illness and disease. You'll read more about this in each pillar's description.

So let's get to it. We'll start with one that is deceptively simple, but exceedingly vital.

## Pillar #1: Hydration

I can't emphasize enough how key proper hydration is to your health. Our weight is approximately 60 percent water. This is because water is essential nearly every function of living.

Here are just a few reasons your body needs water:

- Water helps your body flush away toxins.
- Water helps regulate temperature and maintain other bodily functions.
- Water keeps the tissues in your body moist—including your brain.
- Water helps protect the spinal cord, and it acts as a lubricant and cushion for your joints.
- Water allows the smooth flow of nutrients into the cells.
- Water is essential for proper digestion.
- Water prevents build-up of salts, which can lead to kidney stones.
- Water keeps cells plump and full, which means that your skin will look firmer and clearer (but not "fat").

Dehydration can kill you faster than starvation, which tells us that we need water more than food. But even mild dehydration for a day or so can affect the way we feel and operate. It can give us headaches and nausea, make us feel foggy and fatigued, increase or decrease our appetite, trigger cravings (food, alcohol, drugs, cigarettes, spending), and cause irritability and nervousness.

What's worse is that dehydration is insidious; we often feel these effects before we actually feel thirsty.

Despite all the water bottles you see being toted around, too many of us ignore our basic need for hydration. We rush from place to place, from chore to chore, and forget to refuel. Maybe we grab a coffee to keep going. But we forget just how much water we need. We feel fatigued, groggy, and worse and blame our busy lives, or our age, and so on. We feel sick and want to eat junk but don't know why.

Thankfully the solution is super simple: Drink lots of water.

Because your body loses water through breathing, sweating, and digestion, it's important to rehydrate by drinking fluids and eating foods that contain water. The amount of water you need depends on a variety of factors, including the climate you live in, how physically active you are, and whether you're experiencing an illness or have any other health problems.

Recommendations vary, but according to the Institute of Medicine, the average requirement for women is approximately ½ ounce of water per pound of weight. This means that a 130-pound woman should be drinking 65 ounces of water every day. If you are exercising intensely or it's a hot day, you can up that by at least 50 percent.

I suggest starting your day Kindfully by giving your body what it craves: water. Overnight our bodies dehydrate, often leaving us sluggish or nauseated. Try drinking one to three 10-ounce glasses of water as soon as you wake up. If you have to leave the house quickly or have a long commute, you probably want to stick with one glass. I keep a large glass of water by my bed so it's the very first thing I do when I open my eyes.

To continue drinking enough water throughout the day, I recommend carrying a reusable glass or metal bottle with you. And keep a measurable bottle or pitcher filled at home so you can keep track of your intake until it becomes second nature.

And don't be tricked into thinking that your morning coffee or evening beer counts—it doesn't. In fact, alcoholic drinks and coffee—although they are liquid—actually dehydrate the body. A good alternative to water is tea. Teas contain natural compounds known as polyphenols, which have antioxidant properties. So not only is tea hydrating, it helps protect against numerous diseases.

Foods like fruit, especially melon and cucumber, are very hydrating. Other ways to hydrate include using a humidifier in your bedroom—especially during the winter.

If you start being vigilant about your water intake, you will quickly—possibly overnight—notice improvement in your digestion, mood, skin, and energy, along with changes in appetite (quelling nausea and decreasing cravings).

This pillar will be a big help as you tackle adding—or strengthening—the other pillars, especially the next one.

## Pillar #2: Nutrition

Food, glorious food! Food takes on enormous meaning in each and every culture. In the U.S., for instance, food is used as a reward and treat, it's the focus of intense competition on television shows, the topic of thousands of books and magazines, an intrinsic part of dates, weddings, and birthday celebrations, and it's used as comfort if we're bored, sad, lonely, or worried. It's easy to see why the original importance of food has been overshadowed. But the fact is, food is our fuel and our medicine.

Deep down we all know that eating well is essential for living Kindfully and healthfully, and that the right foods will nourish us and give us energy. But what does eating well mean?

There is no one answer or one diet for everyone because we all have different cultural backgrounds, tastes, and biological needs. For example, eating well for me—a moderately active woman in her 50s—would not work for a young, male athlete. I would gain lots of weight eating his daily requirement of 3,000 calories or more. He might need more protein overall and carbs for quick energy before competitions. And he might not enjoy the exotic foods and spices that I do.

There are folks with allergies and food intolerances, and others who need to avoid certain foods because of chronic conditions like diabetes, kidney disease, and heart problems. That is why I can't give you a prescribed eating plan. There are many ways to find out what your bodily nutritional requirements are based on your health, activity level, gender, and age. You can do some online research, see a doctor, or consult a nutritionist.

That being said, there are general guidelines that benefit all of us:

- Eat three meals a day (or the equivalent in smaller meals) and definitely don't skip breakfast. People who do are more prone to fatigue later in the day and have a harder time meeting their nutritional requirements.

- Meals should have a balance of lean protein, healthy fats, and complex carbohydrates. Examples of lean protein include fish, white meat chicken, tofu, tempeh, beans, and smaller portions of red meat with the fat trimmed (on occasion). Healthy fats include those in nuts, fatty fish like salmon, avocado, and olive and canola oils. And finally, complex carbs are unrefined grains like brown rice, farro, wheatberries, barley, whole grain breads, and whole grain pastas. Starchy vegetables like potatoes and beans have amazing benefits but should be a replacement for grains instead of for leafy green and other vegetables.

- Eat a rainbow. Consuming foods of different colors (red tomatoes, purple beets, blueberries, orange carrots, green broccoli, white mushrooms, yellow peppers, etc.) means we are getting a wide variety of vitamins and minerals. If you aim for at least six servings of diverse fruit and vegetables every day, you will likely have the nutrients your body needs to function at its best and ward off diseases.

- Try your best to prepare meals at home, even if it's just breakfast and occasional dinners. Processed and restaurant-prepared foods are often higher in salt, sugar, and fat.

- When you do eat out, limit fried foods and don't feel like you have to be a member of the clean plate club. If you're served an enormous portion (as in most restaurants these days) ask to take half home. In fact, if you're trying to lose weight, ask for a carryout box and put half away before you dig in.

- Watch your portions. Learn what are proper portion sizes for your age, weight, and activity level. Eat smaller meals and snacks. We don't notice it because we're so accustomed to it, but digestion uses a ton of energy in the body. The more we eat, the more the body needs to rest.

- Avoid foods with too much sugar, rich foods, and foods with empty calories (like chips, pastries, etc.). Instead of nourishing us, these foods will deplete us of energy.

- Finally, and this one is tough for me…slow down. Mealtime is for you. See it as a sacred part of your day—a moment of peace and gratitude. Don't inhale your food. Appreciate each bite and you will protect against overeating and indigestion.

I've just thrown a lot of suggestions at you that may be new or unfamiliar. If this is the case, I suggest trying one or two to start until it becomes habit and moving on to others later. And remember to acknowledge any progress Kindfully. Also, you can check out recipes on my website: www.karenazeezwellbeings.com

These suggestions will help you to lose any unnecessary weight and feel more energized, which will definitely help with the next pillar.

## Pillar #3: Exercise

We all know that there are certain things that we need to do every day to stay alive: breathe, eat, and drink. But did you know that movement also belongs on that list? Physical activity isn't optional for human beings. We are designed to move—not just for optimum health or staying slim—but to actually keep the heart pumping and the blood flowing properly.

Here are the facts: The muscle activity needed for movement triggers important processes related to the breakdown of fats and sugars within the body. When you don't move, these processes stall. Over the long haul, low levels of activity can lead to obesity and metabolic syndrome—a cluster of conditions that includes increased blood pressure, high blood sugar, excess body fat around the waist, and abnormal cholesterol levels.

Any of us who have cared for a sedentary friend or family member knows that lack of exercise adversely affects their chance at recovery and independence. But it can sneak up on all of us, as it did for me. Caretakers and other overly busy, overly responsible folks are particularly vulnerable. We neglect ourselves, get out of shape, and the next thing we know, we fall and we're too weak to get up, perhaps we break a bone, and we're of no use to anyone.

On the flip side, besides protecting us from debilitating accidents, all physical movement has been shown to improve our mood, ease stress, and can even improve libido. The kind of physical exhaustion that comes from exercise practically ensures a good night sleep. Movement aids in digestion, too.

Cardio (running, walking, swimming) is essential for our heart, lungs, and blood flow, while strength training (weights, yoga, Pilates) builds muscle and bone, improves balance, and boosts our metabolism. And it all burns calories.

Most adults should get at least 110 minutes a week of moderate activity like walking, biking, or anything that gets the heart beating faster—keep in mind, that's only a bit over 15 minutes a day! And try to work in two to three session of weight-bearing exercises a week. Believe me, it will make you feel fitter, leaner, and ready to tackle the world.

The hardest part is getting started or starting again after a lapse. I know. I wasn't brought up playing sports nor am I a runner nor drawn to the gym, so I had to find some form of physical movement that worked for me. I tried everything from Aquasize to Zumba. I learned I need something that involves the body, mind, and spirit so I've settled on yoga, hiking, weight training, and, of course, long walks with my dog. If you were not born into an athletic family or it's been a while since you've done anything resembling exercise, how do you start? I work with my clients to help them discover and incorporate fun and easy ways to get active on a regular basis.

You can explore what works for you by thinking about whether you would like exercising at home alone, or in the outdoors, or with companions. You may prefer engaging your spirit, doing something rewarding, or getting competitive. Look back at some of your more satisfying experiences with movement. For example, if you enjoyed tennis as a teen, then start taking lessons again or call a friend, find a court, and play. If you feel good stretching, look into Pilates. If you like learning something new and using your brain, try dance.

Here's some more inspiration:

- Get a 30-day pass to a comprehensive gym and try a new kind of class every other day.

- Take dance lessons.

- Check out the myriad workout DVDs, apps, and free YouTube videos to try workouts at home.

- If it's winter, ski, snowboard, or go snowshoeing or ice skating.

- Try stripper pole workouts to make exercise seem "naughty" instead of "good."

- Gather friends to play touch football in the park.
- Join a bowling or volleyball league.
- Volunteer to walk dogs in a shelter.
- Bike to work.
- Walk to work.
- Go horseback riding.
- Go rowing or kayaking.
- Take walking tours of your city.
- Learn a martial art like Tai Chi or Karate.

Go forward and exercise Kindfully. That means learning what your body likes and giving yourself loving encouragement to try to pursue what's good for you. It will definitely help for the next pillar.

## Pillar #4: Stress Management

Stress is a lot like death and taxes—it's inevitable (and definitely not fun!).

If you have a job, you may have stress from deadlines, coworkers' feuds, the boss's miscommunication, long commutes, failing technology, and more. If you are in a relationship, you may have conflicts over money, space, and time. If you have family, you strive to balance responsibilities and expectations on a daily basis. And those are just the big three stressors. I could list a dozen more off the top of my head.

Unless we decide to shed all our worldly goods and spend our remaining days as monks, we're going to have to learn to deal with stress before stress deals with us. The thing is, stress—even for short periods of time—can hurt our bodies, moods, and behavior quickly and deeply. Here are just a few ways:

Common effects of stress on your body

- Headache
- Muscle tension or pain
- Chest pain
- Fatigue
- Change in sex drive
- Stomach upset
- Sleep problems
- High blood pressure

Common effects of stress on your mood

- Anxiety
- Restlessness
- Lack of motivation or focus
- Feeling overwhelmed
- Irritability or anger
- Sadness or depression

Common effects of stress on your behavior

- Overeating or undereating
- Angry outbursts
- Drug or alcohol abuse
- Tobacco use
- Social withdrawal
- Exercising less often

During especially stressful times, I can feel stress chipping away at my health: My appetite disappears and then comes back with a salty-sugary vengeance; I feel worn out but wired; I'm foggy—even dizzy; I become irritable and impatient.

Thankfully, when we practice Kindfulness, we can feel the effects of stress, identify the cause, and apply the techniques we've learned to minimize any damage. Many of the aspects of cultivating self-compassion described in Chapter 4 can be used to alleviate stress. They include:

- Lightening the Load
- Compassionate Self-Talk
- Affirmations
- Gratitude
- Spirituality
- Fun

Many of the techniques to cultivate mindfulness offered in Chapter 2 are incredibly useful in reducing stress. They include:

- Breathwork
- Meditation (all forms)
- Grounding
- Reality Checks

In addition (and this is when the pillars become more of a circle of life), ensure that you eat properly, drink enough water (remember, dehydration can cause irritability and nervousness), and exercise. Getting that heart pumping is perhaps—along with meditation—the greatest stress buster out there!

Here are even more suggestions for handling stress:

### Create a Safe Space

We all need and deserve time and space to wind down and feel safe. This will mean something different for each person. For me, it's having a clean, neat, organized home. For others, it might mean having a room to themselves or—conversely—having friends and loved ones around. Whether it involves music, candles, scented oils, or your favorite blanket, find or create a place that makes you feel comforted and gives you the opportunity to let down without feeling exposed.

## Escape for a While

Being in a crisis often means nonstop stimuli, which is an all-out assault on our nervous system and sends hormones like cortisol into fight or flight mode. This can do a lot of damage if not nipped in the bud. If you can take a break, take one. In fact, even if you feel like you can't, ask for help to make it happen. Pop in your favorite movie, sit in a park or garden, or take a long bath. If you're involved in a long-term crisis, consider taking a weekend or week off and going away. It's not selfish, it's your survival plan.

## Do Something

Often in stressful times we feel out of control, helpless, and hopeless. We're waiting for test results, for a loved one to come home safely, or we open bills we can't pay. The worst thing you can do is to do nothing. Sitting and ruminating, having negative thoughts go around and around only magnifies the problem. Instead, get up and do something productive or positive. Maybe it's cleaning your home or calling a friend who is also struggling and just listening to them. Give the dog a long-overdue bath, organize a closet or old photos, or give yourself a pedicure. Just take action that will keep your mind engaged and make you feel like you've accomplished something.

Unfortunately, living life and loving others will often mean we suffer some sort of calamity now and then. Taking care of ourselves during this time is a vital aspect of living Kindfully. It is not only the best thing we can do for ourselves, but for everyone else involved.

And finally, to keep stress at a tolerable level, we must get proper sleep. Stress can cause a vicious cycle: Anxiety prevents us from sleeping long and deeply and then lack of sleep makes us feel more anxious and irritable and unable to handle stress.

Not surprisingly, that brings us to the fifth and final pillar.

## Pillar #5: Sleep

You're well hydrated, you've eaten well but not too much, you've exercised, relaxed, and laughed, so you should sleep like a baby, right? Well, those actions will definitely promote good, sound sleep, but many of us have chronic sleep issues that aren't as easily solved and affect our everyday lives.

This seemingly simple part of life can be a nightmare for millions of people. Nearly 70 million Americans report having a sleep issue, and roughly 40 percent of adults get less than the recommended minimum amount of sleep each night. It's really a national crisis.

At the core of this issue is a big chunk of denial. Most of us don't even realize we have a problem. We're just used to spending half our days in a daze, tossing and turning at night, or feeling cranky and unmotivated. We think it's just part of life. But it's not part of living Kindfully.

Just a night or two of lousy sleep can affect the areas of the brain that control impulses, imagination, and our abilities to incorporate new information. Despite what we're taught, this puts us at a serious disadvantage at work. There's still an attitude in our culture that surviving on a small amount of sleep is a badge of honor and makes you kind of an office hero. Well, it doesn't. Those who get a proper amount of sleep are actually superior workers. According to an article in Inc. Magazine, studies have shown they have better concentration and memory, are more insightful and creative, and are just easier to get along with.

And it's not just at the office. Lack of sleep makes us crabby spouses, impatient friends, and, in some cases, can lead to very dangerous sleep disorders.

Proper sleep also helps balance ghrelin and leptin, two hormones that regulate hunger and appetite satiety. Lack of sleep can lead to serious carb cravings the next day, and over time can cause major weight gain and diabetes.

We all want deeper, longer sleep without drugs. I'm here to tell you it is possible with a few tweaks to your habits and home environment. For example:

### Limit Caffeine

It may take some trial and error to find the sweet spot of how much caffeine is too much, but a good rule of thumb is to stop caffeine intake (this includes tea and cola) after 3 p.m.

### Get Moving

Even if it's just a 20-minute walk, some form of physical exertion is crucial to give us the physical exhaustion that leads to proper sleep.

### Monitor your Meals

You may want to skip large, heavy meals or extra spicy foods a few hours before bedtime. I need to pass on Kung Pao Tofu with Szechuan peppers at 9 p.m. Now I reserve large or spicy meals for earlier in the evening. Late-night suppers need to be lighter or blander if I'm going to sleep like a baby.

### Cut off Drinking

Hydration is super important, but getting up two to three times to pee in the middle of the night can affect your sleep cycles and duration of sleep. Not good. Cut off all drinks at least one hour before bedtime. This includes a nightcap. Alcohol may help you fall asleep but it disrupts sleep later on.

### No Late-Night Business

Focusing on work keeps the brain awake and can cause anxiety. Set a time when the business day is done and try not to open mail or bills after regular office hours. Why find out you were overcharged at 10 p.m. when you can't call to rectify it until 9 a.m.? Resist "one last check" of email before bed—unless that check will reassure you.

## Don't Oversleep

It's tempting to lay in bed for a couple of extra hours when exhausted or after a night of disrupted sleep, but this means that you'll likely have trouble falling asleep at your normal bedtime…which means that you'll want to sleep late again, and so on. Instead, soldier through the day until it's time to sink in to that glorious pillow again.

## Tweak Your Bedroom

Creating a cool, dark, quiet, and relatively neat room promotes proper sleep. Investing in a quality mattress, sheets, and pillows along with room-darkening or noise-dampening window treatments can also dramatically improve slumber. You can also try sound machines. Removing all electronics (yes, even the TV and smartphone!) from your bedroom and clearing away clutter improves your chances of a good night's sleep immeasurably. Blue light emitted from electronic devices mimics daylight and tells our brains to wake up, not drift off.

## Develop a Sleep Routine

Doing the same pre-bedtime activities night after night sends an unconscious message to the brain that it's time to shut down. About 45 minutes to an hour before bed, I plug in my phone to charge, tidy up a bit, put on my PJs, brush my teeth, wash and moisturize my face, bring in my glass of water to the nightstand, pull down the bedcovers, call in the dog, and read. After 20 minutes or so of a good book or magazine, I can't keep my eyes open.

## Get the Right Light

Exposing yourself to light in the morning helps reset circadian rhythms by lowering melatonin levels. The type of light matters, as does the length of exposure. Direct sunlight outdoors for at least 30 minutes produces the most benefit.

## Affirmations and Breathwork

If you wake up in the middle of the night with anxiety and can't fall back asleep, try some of the breathwork and soothing talk/affirmations described in previous chapters. The middle of the night can be a scary place, so reality checks are also helpful in these situations to assure yourself that everything is OK.

These suggestions may or may not apply to you, and that's because we're all different when it comes to our sleep obstacles, needs, and preferences. Add to that different work schedules, diets, living situations, and so on, and you can see why sleeping Kindfully isn't a one-size-fits-all situation. If you are having trouble sleeping, try one or two and then move on until you find the right fit.

## Putting it All Together

If you've noticed redundancies in this book, if I've mentioned meditation, breathing, and focusing on yourself a dozen or more times, for instance, it means that it is integral to living Kindfully and using the Kindfulness Solution to achieve your goals. Meditation helps with stress, reducing stress helps with energy, energy allows us to exercise, exercise helps reduce stress, and so on. The concepts within this book all work together, but are often not linear. They are more circular.

That is why I stress using this book as you see fit, as it works just for you. But it's not just to be read, it is to be done. Just as watching an exercise show will not burn calories, reading this book without attempting its assignments and suggestions will only avail you of some knowledge. Knowledge without action can't effect lasting or significant change. That's the truth.

I also can't recommend doing this alone. As I outlined in previous chapters, it is vital to include friends, family, coworkers, social media followers, doctors, therapists, or others in this journey. None of us live in a vacuum and all of us can benefit from support and accountability.

And for my overachievers out there…

Maybe you started reading this book with grand plans to turn your life around in a month. Then maybe you got stuck. It happens. That's because grand plans are difficult and often overwhelming. You think they require monumental, dramatic sweeping changes—but actually it's the opposite. It's all about taking small, simple steps and committing to a life-long pursuit of wellness.

Rocky didn't become a champ overnight. He had to run up all those steps and punch a lot of meat (yuck!). But first he had to make a decision to learn to box, then find a trainer, then buy some gray sweats, and so on. When we break down change this way it seems a lot less overwhelming and totally doable.

We're never going to do it all and do it perfectly. We are all unique creatures put on this earth to have our one-of-a-kind journey. My book is just a tool to help you make the best of that journey, the best of the body you have, the best life that you would want for yourself.

While some want fame and fortune, others are content to be the best friend or parent they can be.  Some of you will try to lose weight, train to run a marathon, try to quit smoking, learn yoga, start home cooking, go back to school. But few of us can do all that at once—or even in a lifetime. You choose your direction, you decide how you make your mark in this life—no one else can make those decisions.

Once you've chosen a path, keep this book by your side. Think of me— and millions of others like us who are venturing to finally live the life that they deserve—by your side. We're with you as you get out of bed to hit the gym. We're with you as you stay busy to fend off a cigarette or doughnut craving. We're with you as you take brave steps to say no and delegate some responsibilities.

Hear my voice in your head sending you encouragement, support, and love. That is until you can replace my voice with your own. Until you can find your own inner Kindfulness.

Be well, be brave, and be as Kindful to yourself as you can.

*Check out the "about the author" section of this book to learn how to sign up for my weekly newsletter, stay connected on social media, and learn about workshops and other events.*

# ACKNOWLEDGMENTS

In this book, you will hear me preach again and again that in order to show yourself compassion and achieve your goals, you will need a team of supporters. I'm proud to say that in writing this book I listened to my own advice, and I am deeply grateful to my team.

First, always, I want to thank my uniquely wonderful husband, Steve, who continues to teach me more about love than I knew was possible, helps me to appreciate everything about myself, and encourages me to follow my dreams no matter how it affects our lives, schedules, or dinner plans.

I couldn't have been more fortunate than to have my dear friend Alison Hall, an accomplished writer and editor, apply her mastery to the editing of my manuscript. I knew her keen eye, diligence, insight, and caring heart were the perfect prerequisites for the job—and I was right! But more than that, she was a true partner in making my message fuller and clearer than I had imagined.

It was truly a gift to be able to include the artistic talents of my niece, Julia Bennett, who provided the amazing illustrations included at the start of each chapter. And I thank her for understanding my vision and learning some technical aspects along the way with patience and enthusiasm.

Frances Rosario-Puleo, my peer coach, was invaluable in providing the push I needed and accountability along the way, in addition to being a cheerleader for my ideas and writing.

And, finally, to all my clients and newsletter readers who continue to inspire me with their courage, candor, and willingness to live the life they deserve. I thank you for walking this path with me.

# ABOUT THE AUTHOR

Karen Azeez is a certified Integrative Nutrition Health Coach, wellness expert, and freelance writer. She received her undergraduate degree at Colgate University and completed her advanced study at New York University's Wellness Program and the Institute for Integrative Nutrition.

She helps busy men and women incorporate simple lifestyle changes to regain their vitality, lose weight, find a fitness routine they enjoy, sleep better, manage stress, and prepare and eat healthy and delicious meals. She offers personalized, one-on-one health coaching sessions, group programs, and workshops on nutrition, health, support for caretakers, and natural beauty. She is in demand as a public speaker in addition to being a featured writer for several health and nutrition websites, and publishes a popular weekly newsletter.

Karen is a native New Yorker living in Manhattan with her husband, Steve, and beloved dog, Rollo. In her spare time, she loves to develop new, healthy recipes, take long walks with her dog, practice yoga, and spend time with friends.

For more information on her recipes, workshops, newsletters, and coaching services, visit her website: www.karenazeezwellbeings.com

Or follow her on social media:

Twitter: @karenazeeznyc

Facebook: https://www.facebook.com/karenazeezwellbeings